Author of the bestseller *365 Days of Happiness*

JACQUELINE PIRTLE

WHAT IT MEANS TO BE A WOMAN

AND YES, WOMEN DO POOP!

ISBN-13: 978-1-7320851-4-5

Published by: FreakyHealer

Credits:

Author: Jacqueline Pirtle

Editor-in-chief: Zoe Pirtle

Editor/layout: Mitch Pirtle

Book cover design by Kingwood Creations
kingwoodcreations.com

Author photo courtesy of Lionel Madiou
madiouART.com

Hair Styling by Alejandro Jimenez
@alejandrojimenezofficial (IG)

DEDICATION

I dedicate this book to all beautiful women in
the whole wide world, especially the ones that
are such an inspiration to me—and that IS you,
my most precious daughter Zoe Pirtle! I love
you to the stars and back.

CONTENTS

ACKNOWLEDGEMENTS

The most incredible creations happen when a beautiful team pulls together! Thank you for your dedication to make this book tangible. I give my appreciation to Zoe Pirtle for her editorial mastery; Mitch Pirtle for his editorial and layout love; kingwoodcreations.com for their fun and polished book cover design; madiouART.com for an amazing photo shoot; and @alejandrojimenezofficial (IG) for his masterful hair design.

I also would like to give a huge "Thank You!" to everyone and everything who urged me to write this important next book, and to all who are always supporting me.

And from the bottom of my heart… Much love to my incredible husband; Mitch Pirtle, my phenomenal children; Zoe Pirtle and Till Pirtle, and our sweet cats… Your constant support and believing in me made this book possible—not to mention the infinite love, laughter, and smiles you are showering me with every single day. Thank you! I love you to the moon and back.

A WORD BY THE AUTHOR

I hope you enjoy this book as much as I loved writing it. If you do, it would be wonderful if you could take a short minute and leave a review on Amazon.com and Goodreads.com as soon as you can, as your kind feedback is much appreciated and so very important. Thank you!

I also want to let you know that I have published two other best-selling books: *365 Days of Happiness*, a day-by-day guide to being happy, and *Parenting Through the Eyes of Lollipops*, a guide for parents to get cracking on "mindful parenting"—a powerful tool for parents and a clear voice for children. Both support the teachings of *What it Means to BE a Woman* and help people, parents, and children to BE and live happier—a cause that is very dear to my heart.

All my books are available wherever books are sold, online on amazon.com, amazon-worldwide, and at www.freakyhealer.com.

365 Days of Happiness is also available as a companion mobile application for both Android and iPhone and can be supplemented with the appropriate self-study program that you can find at www.freakyhealer.com.

For any questions you might have and for more information on my sessions, workshops, presentations, and what ever else I am up to, visit my website www.freakyhealer.com and my social media accounts @freakyhealer.

"If you could see yourself as I see you, you would realize the incredible star that you ARE and not hold back anything anymore. Instead you would BE and live openly, freely, and wildly as the true 'hotness,' as the true woman, that you ARE."
~ Jacqueline Pirtle, your utmost fan

To "**BE** and **Live**" is something that I reference a lot in all my books:

With **BE**, I mean you are being your whole YOU—your body, mind, soul, and consciousness. With **Live**, I mean you are experiencing your physicality—your physical life.

MEET AND GREET

Just like when you start your new dream job and meet your new co-worker who tells you all about the what, why, who, and when, I want you to meet me so I can tell you what I AM all about.

NICE TO MEET YOU

Hi! I am Jacqueline Pirtle, the author of this book. It's really nice to meet you!

Thanks for picking it up. I know that we will have a marvelous time together as women.

Believe me when I say, "I wrote this jewel with my deepest excitement," because I really, really, really, love being a woman. Seriously! Consciously finding the meaning behind "being a woman," made my already-thrilled female existence even more exciting—to the point that I AM feeling on top of the highest mountain about being my own woman.

I hope that this book will get you there too, so we can both - together, throughout our hand-in-hand time - celebrate our femininity, sharing and spreading this elegance with women all around the world.

I was inspired to give writing a try rather by accident, or better said through listening to my oh-so insistent soul-voice, which on New Year's Eve of 2016 was ordering me to write every day of 2017 about happiness. What does happiness mean for me and the world? What IS happiness anyways? And how do you create happiness on a day-to-day or even on a split-second to split-second basis?

At first, it was simply an idea that felt like loads of fun. Then these writings turned into a blog on my website, **freakyhealer.com**, until I got word from readers that they awaited my happiness passages to use as tools to shift themselves into well-being and a state of stable mental health on a daily basis.

That's when it hit me like a lightning bolt—the idea to make a whole book out of these writings so that people can have a little piece of me, and my happiness findings, in their homes and feel good anywhere at anytime; every single day, no matter their circumstances.

The end of December in 2017 came around pretty fast, and even though my lack of knowledge about the book-making business made it daunting at first, it was time for me to become a published author. On December 31st 2017, I gave my book to the editors, found the perfect book cover, went for a photo shoot, edited and rewrote it a million times, and voila—self-published **365 Days of Happiness** in February 2018. This was a successful team effort thanks to the supportive help of many glorious people—for details see the credits. A dream team, indeed!

What an experience! Actually, it was so epic that I decided to write my next book - **Parenting Through the Eyes of Lollipops**, which was self-published in September 2019 - again, with the help of my dream team.

By now I am very much breathing, living, and thinking like a writer—if that is actually a thing. Some say this means that whatever you say could end up on paper, so be careful what you chitter chatter around me... Just kidding!

Besides writing books, I am the owner of the lifestyle company **FreakyHealer**, where I am a holistic practitioner and a speaker. I have been helping clients to live better-feeling lives through my sessions, programs, workshops, and teachings professionally since 2006. Way before that, I helped people on a private level.

My life-long gift of sensing people's energetic needs and situations, then translating that information into words and sharing that crucial wisdom for them to grasp and apply to their lives, has helped thousands of people - privately and professionally - all over the world.

Some call me the brightest light - bright in the sense of shining - in the shed because I grasp momentums that are like open portals, let them vividly flow through me, and deliver said information to the person of interest—always letting me have and give an explanation, hint, or answer.

When living close with me - I'm talking about my family here - it can come across as being an always knowing smart aleck and can be very annoying at times, but for my clients this always knowing is crucial, helpful, and welcomed because they pay me and expect me to consistently know for them—so I give my best to BE and live openly to receive the always knowing wisdom that is there for me to translate to them. This is a very potent way to live life.

How I write is no different—I open up to these portals that are filled with wisdom, let the words flow through me, and on they go into my laptop and onto paper. I know that I am meant to write them because I feel amazing when I do, and that well-feeling of mine is charging my books energetically with potent goodness, which touches your heart deeply. Some readers report back to me that simply looking at, holding, or hugging my books shifts them to well-being before even reading a word.

Privately, I am a happy wife of millions of amazing years to the love of my life and a fulfilled mom to two phenomenal young adults - My children! I always will like to call them my children - and to cats as well—some came and went and never will be forgotten, and some came and are still here, their energy always being on my mind.

As a woman who has lived in this lifetime for quite a while now, I have done millions of the women things that we females are so famous for doing and being, including:

- Figuring out my beautiful female body—continuously learning about all boob and vagina knowledge

- Finding my sexuality—every day, newly and freshly

- Came clean with loving my oh-so always seemingly present and never-really-ending period—since it's not just when it's flowing, but way before and way after, that it makes a mark on my body and mood

- Becoming a mom—two kids made it and one did not

- Finding my strengths and weaknesses—if there really is such a thing as weakness

- Setting boundaries—more and more clearly as I go

- Cleansing out my old recordings, habits, and beliefs of needing to be a "good girl"

- Feeling beautiful about myself as a whole

- Falling in love with myself, followed by really unconditionally loving myself anew and anew

- Celebrating the sometimes-absence of my period, and loving my beautifully mature age—figuring this gracious phase of being a woman out as I go

I know that I have done "enough" experiences of being a woman in order to gracefully write this book about the meaning of being a woman, and give respect to the power of what being a woman really means. Not only am I happy being a woman, I am also very positive in my beautiful female garden where all sorts of feminine plants are growing—beautiful flowers (experiences) right beside all the weeds of rape, sexual abuse, physical and emotional abuse, and the realness of experiencing that for some people, a woman is of lesser value; or that my red hair means I am a witch to some to this day.

In nature, flowers and weeds all together make the most gorgeous garden ever. Many times the weeds actually feed and fuel the flowers to grow more beautiful, strong, and powerful than ever—enough to weather any storm. You as a woman are no different!

Now, it is of absolute importance to me that you stop all compassion, empathy, or identifying yourself with my mentioned traumas immediately - if that is where you were heading - because not only am I not fishing for your heartfelt sympathy, it is of no value to you and me if you step into the lake of feeling them for me. If this puts the big question mark of "What's that all about?" on your forehead, I want you to jump to the chapter **Compassion and Empathy** *- yes, I wrote a whole chapter about these two very important feelings - with speed. There I explain how* *to feel those feelings in a good-feeling way—the only way, really. I promise, you will see that I am no cold-hearted woman because of what I just said.*

Don't get me wrong, when things happen against our will it is brutal and can be unforgivable. I never endorse that behavior or happening ever. The offender needs to be held accountable, and the victim needs support, love, and unlimited never-ending respect.

However, there IS humongous healing possible in these traumas and wounds—as well as an invitational growth opportunity of self-love. I decided early on to claim it all, that I am not a victim and won't spread and share victim energy—even if it is available for me to choose from. Instead, turn it all around to be my own empower-er, and from that healthy space I share and spread absolute empowerment. For me, empowering is far more helpful than "victim-ing"—with everything that life has in store to be experienced.

I have not mentioned my wounds before publicly—not because I feel shame or want to hide them, but simply out of love for the constant forward-moving state by not focusing or dwelling on the old. Running around and talking about what happened, to every cell I encounter, would represent that re-live, re-create, and re-feel of these old happenings again and again. All while the world grows compassion and empathy for me, maybe even builds a monument for all that I have been through—shifting the focus away from my work of helping people live happier lives, to the world talking about my traumas and feeling sorry for me. This is a momentum that I don't judge, but am not seeking, because it simply is not my cup of tea and in the end won't help me or the people that love my teachings.

"But why now?" you might ask.

Now is the fitting time for me to share it in a way that is right for me, because this book is about and for women—and also about and for me. Plus, I didn't want you to be part of my old problematic experiences, I wanted you to be a witness of my new amplified solutions—and now I want to help you through what I calibrated into because of it all. The intention of this book and all my teachings IS to shift anything and everything to BE an empowering experience to have—meaning to shift being a woman into an empowering experience to have. No matter the circumstances.

And with that, let the big, bold, curtains fall and the glorious stage for this empowering play of **What it Means To BE a Woman** begin—to be witnessed by, shared with, and spread to ALL women: young and old, small and big; slim or voluptuous; lesbian or straight, transgender or cisgender; decided or undecided of their femininity, married or single; mother or not, homestay or career-oriented; rich or poor, healthy or unhealthy; disabled or not, short-haired or longhaired, hairy or no hair, and of any and all religions.

To ALL women, of the whole wide world—you ladies rock!

You ALL have my purest acknowledgment, my deepest respect, my finest appreciation, my full-on gratitude, and my sincere love.

Not leaving men out on purpose, you have my deepest respect too, but after all—this IS a book about and for women.

Yours truly, Jacqueline

All views in this book are my own opinions and experiences—take what fits from it and leave the rest behind. Only you know what is best for you!

With utmost certainty, I never endorse any form of overstepping, abuse, or bullying towards women, or anyone or anything. If needed get help for yourself and for others. You deserve only the best and so does everyone else.

Be kind. Be smart. Be helpful. Be real. *Be a good person!*

REALLY QUICK BEFORE WE GET STARTED

So... What does it mean to BE a woman?

Being a woman means to claim your energetic essence and your female energy, compile it into one, and focus that powerful, classy, and elegant energetic force into your female physical body—then exhilarate it to such a level of concentration that you show up in your physical life as who you came here to BE. Furthermore, to radically live as that, all the while constantly expanding more and more, bigger and bigger, into the calibration that you are meant to transition into over your lifetime. So when it is transition time, your physical you is satisfied and can say, "I did it! Congratulations to me! On to more now..."

That's it! This is what it means to BE your woman!

You know so much and in such clarity now that you don't even need to keep reading this book. Just kidding—again! Gosh, do I love sarcasm...

I know that you want to know the "how" to do exactly that of what I just talked about, so keep reading and let's go!

Be kind. Be smart. Be helpful. Be real. *Be a good person!*

THE STORY BEHIND THE SUBTITLE: AND YES, WOMEN DO POOP!

Let's clear the air first because to me, clarity wins every single time! I was on the fence on whether to put that subtitle on the front of the book because in my head I was thinking "Really? *Poop* gets the front seat on my new book?" But after many sleepless nights and tossing and turning while at it...

Back in time, I overheard a conversation between young ladies, talking about young men who don't think that women poop. Did I really believe that? Well, it did seem somewhat impossible that people would think the bodies of women don't have that bodily function—but then again, who am I to say?

This got me thinking, that even if the "not knowing" of those young men might not be meant literally, it still is a stigma that such bodily functions are not lady-like—whereas men can talk and laugh about them loudly and freely and are even glorified as strong heroes when farting out loud or talking about monster-sized poops. Women, on the other hand, are quieted by zip your lips and do not mention them; that the pooping business was gross and an unspeakable thing for girls, yet ok for boys. This was a fact when I was growing up, and it seems that to this day it is still a gigantic elephant in the room for some—all because it was, and still is, existing as those old beliefs in society.

For me, having had children of my own, taught me to loosen up and shift my old imprinted grossness-thoughts around to a new, normal, and healthy, "poop is phenomenal" belief—creating a wonderful resistance-free and very healthy environment for me to BE, live in, and experience with my children. So thanks, kids, for helping me with that! My whole being, especially my physical body, is very happy that way.

That was enough of a reason - without further investigating the truth of the beliefs of those young men - to give this subtitle a front seat and make it very visible on my book. My thought was that even if someone does not pick up my book, just seeing the cover can be the needed reminder, eye-opener, or thought-inspiration, starring them straight in the eye that:

- Women do go number two—poop

- It is natural, normal, and healthy that women poop

- Women do have all these body functions that are not always considered to be of a "pretty, beautiful, and gracious" nature by society

- We can talk about all body functions normally

In truth, pooping is very pretty, incredibly beautiful, and infinitely gracious—it keeps you *pretty* healthy, *beautifully* slim, and *graciously* smooth moving. Plus, have you ever looked at poop close-up? Pretty impressive stuff!

I want to make this truth very public, and bury all untruths about this subject to be cleared forever—it's very important to me!

So…

This is a great reminder for all women, young and old, for every parent to a female, and for all men in the whole world, that women are not here in this physical life to impress or bless anyone besides themselves with prettiness, beauty, and graciousness—especially not through the fabricated old-style expectation of not having these body functions just because they don't hold up the honor medal of "female beauty."

And for giggles, since poop is in fact included in the package deal of what a woman is and in truth is very pretty, beautiful, and gracious - as we covered above - you would not want to expect women to impress and bless you with all their beauty, because that could get crappy really fast—not the pretty picture that some expect it to be.

It is also a reality check for all women who are not in love with their body functions that pooping, farting, burping, sweating like a dog, and stinking, is in fact normal and has to happen in order for your physical body to be healthy and exist—so that you get to experience this physical life in the good company of your thriving body.

My hopes are that this subtitle brings forth a stop to any humiliation from body functions, by reminding the world to let go of any false shame that is put on women and humanity as a whole—besides creating giggles for those who already knew that secret, and as a sassy eye-catcher for people to pick up my book.

I really hope that you share this chapter with all women— be it your daughter, your friend, or a stranger that you see struggling with realizing the prettiness, beauty, and graciousness of her body functions.

I also really hope that you share it with all of the men in your life; husbands, sons, and sons of mom-friends. It can literally change the understanding and the treatment of all women in the world—creating an unstoppable uplift in the experience of relationships between all women and men.

Plus don't forget... Think about the well-deserved respect poop gets from you talking freely and normally about it. And by all means, if you must, go freely about your body noises. I know of quite a few ladies who swear up and down that it is freeing for them to fart and burp as it comes, not to mention the giggles it initiates—and with common sense, you should be safe doing so.

Now that the awkwardness has left the book, let's dive deep into more intimate topics together.

Be kind. Be smart. Be helpful. Be real. *Be a good person!*

THE BASICS

In order for us to really enjoy our time together in this book - I like to pretend that you reading my book means we are spending a wonderful time together - and as fellow human beings, we need to find common ground, like syncing up with each other.

LET'S GET CLEAR AND CONNECT

I am coming, just like you, from the non-physical into this physicality of existence. Most people say that I am super sensitive and always was—as a child they did not always know what to do about me and my constantly unable-to-see-through-the-physical-eye ways that instigated my reactions. The explanation to this is that I was always very strongly energetically wired—always very connected to my inner self. I mean, we all are, but some of us are a billion times more delicate in living and feeling our lives. I sensed and perceived everything and everyone very intensely through my energetic level first, and only secondly did I then experience what was going on in a physical life way—and was able to put one-and-one together to understand and make others understand too. My strong "sensing" arrived in different ways; strong feelings, deep visions, and profound thoughts. This is also true today, just very magnified and infinitely more educated by now.

As an example; if you speak to me, I sense your energy and the energetic value of your words way before acknowledging the meaning of the spoken words. I read by sensing the energy of the words and the energy of the writer first, and only then do I notice the written meaning of them. If you play music, I sense the vibration of that music before listening to the sound, and I sense the energy of someone singing and the composer of that song way before hearing what the words really mean. I sense the energy of food and decide if that energy is good for me and is a match for my nutritional needs before choosing what to eat. I sense someone's energy, and in which frequency they are vibrating in, no matter if they are near or far.

That is why I am able to help people even if they are not physically here with me—I get out of my physicality and hang out with everything and everyone on the energetic level first, a field of consciousness that has no limits and is formless and infinite. Only after do I shift into the realm of physical life, and honestly, most of the time once I arrive on the physical level nothing makes sense to me—but that is a whole new book right there.

Why is this infinitely profound?

Because there are two essences that make up your existence in your physical life. There is your physical you, made of your physical body experiencing physical life on this physical earth, and there is your energetic essence—the non-physical, your soul, that is a part of you that never dies but always IS.

Then there is your whole being that is existing here on earth as a complex mass—made of different components; your physical body, your mind, your non-physical soul, and this field of consciousness that you are part of and ONE with.

I believe that the non-physical part is the biggest part of me—bigger than my physical me, smarter than my physical me, and more important than my physical me. I also believe that I am living this physical life from my bigger non-physical part, and not the other way around. I also know that I AM here to expand in my energetic essence, and that this expansion brings everything and everyone further along in their reasons as to why they are here and who they really are. I love the fact that I put my focus mostly on my energetic essence in order to experience the whole of my physical life fully, because it has no limits, whereas physicality does.

The good news for you, and everyone else, is that there is nothing special about me being first and foremost energetically wired because you are too—everyone IS. Everyone is the same as me, an energetic essence and a physical essence. It is as that whole complex being that we are here to experience physical life and expand in our energy—which we share and enrich everyone and everything.

The special part is really only in how I perceive everything in physical life, which is first from the energetic viewpoint—versus most people who are living firstly from their physical realm and at some point maybe, shift to experience from their energetic essence because of some good or bad happenings.

You might say, "Alrighty, but what's to say that your way is a better way?"

First off, I think that the best way for everyone is to follow their happiness and to make sure that their priority is to feel good in physical life. Nobody knows better about what is good or better for you, than you. So, is my way better than yours? I don't know, you tell me!

A lot of times people don't know what is best for them or they live their lives sort of muted until something good or bad happens, ripping them out of their normal physical life ways. That is when realizing that you are a complex being - a body, mind, soul, and one with consciousness - living a complex life, made of a manifested physical part and also an energetic component, is of real value. That is also the time when your best answers lie in your energetic essence and float to the surface if you pay attention, because physical life and your physical body has limits—whereas in the energetic realm, there are no limits and no restrictions. That right there could be your answer to why experiencing firstly as your energetic being is a better way.

Fact is that we, everything, and everyone are all the same— energy! As such, we are eternal energetic essences - soul beings - that choose to come here to have free and always available access to limitless guidance and wisdom in the field of consciousness. We are here to live a physical life that is filled with wisdom and knowing, for our soul passion and soul journeys to be completed.

You ARE energetically wired! Your cables are laid and there is never a shortage of energy but always enough for all! You just have to plug in!

If you think of energy, it is only normal to think of it as constantly vibrating, moving, changing, shifting, and expanding—making all your energetic essence, your physical existence, and physical life a constant-moving and ever-changing entity. Nothing ever stays the same!

As these energies we are here to expand by experiencing and learning about physical life and humanity as a whole. Every happening, thought, word, feeling, encounter, and moving around in your life - these are all energies too - gives you the expansion that you came here to create and share with the whole world and beyond. You chose to come here to expand in exactly such ways.

To recap:

• Energy is all there IS

• We, everything, and everyone are all the same energy

• Energy is constantly vibrating and moving—some at higher or lower frequencies

• Higher frequencies are feel-good experiences and lower ones are of unwell feeling nature

• All energy carries certain information—some of higher value than others

• Everyone as a whole consists of part physical and part energetic essence

• The physical is energy that manifested into the physical— body, physical life, physical things

• The energetic is your soul, your mind, the field of consciousness, and all that has not manifested into the physical yet

• We are connected as one in this field of consciousness

• We share our energies at all times

• You can change your energetic value, information, and the frequency you are vibrating in at any moment—you are 100% in charge

Here is one more example before we move on to the next vividly shifting chapter: Writing my books and practicing my holistic work is so successful because I am most and foremost energetically present in order to get all the information from the energetic space, the non-physical, the field of consciousness, to translate it into a manifestation of words, explanations, and information for you to grasp and apply in a physical life way—with your mind, which is fully energetic, mind you!

This makes it a rock-solid knowing that I am given these words to write for you, and the complete trust that they are right for me to write. That is also why it feels so cleansing and happifying for me to do my sacred work, and for my readers and clients to follow my teachings.

Be kind. Be smart. Be helpful. Be real. *Be a good person!*

STARTING OUT AS EQUALS

We all start out the same: as energy! Nobody is different, more, or has increased special-ness than someone else. This is an important fact to remember, to keep this mob of energies - present and future ladies and gentlemen - under control in this physical world.

Think about it: Equality at its best, right from the start and THE natural way of how it, everything, and everyone IS—meaning we don't have to create equality, it already IS.

That is until…

We arrive here in this physical world by following the choice of our non-physical essence to come, either as a woman or a man which, by the way, clearly shows which part of us is the boss by being the decision maker. Our non-physical energetic essence! That puts the tip of the sword straight towards who you should be asking anything that you want to know about yourself, your life, and your purpose here.

You really did choose to come here and BE a woman— versus kinda sorta stumbling through the door of physicality and showing up as such. That is worth recognizing and celebrating, even if later in your life journey you choose to change your sex. The point here is that you deliberately arrived as a woman, complete with a physical female body, a mind, soul, soul guidance, soul passion, and soul journey that is one with consciousness—with the clear plan in mind to further expand in your physical life as that female body, or whatever you choose to be, as you get to know yourself better.

The moment you stepped through this gate-to-earth is the point in time where your fresh and new mind gets filled with only in-physical-life-existing, made-up, and flawed, beliefs that lots of currently living minds keep holding onto—that one is more than the other, that men are more than women, that children are less than adults, or that skin color matters. In the situation of gender, the rules of inequality are because men and women are different in physicality, different physical bodies and different physical capabilities. Add to that the different thoughts, feelings, likes, and expectations.

Generations after generations operating like this is what is keeping this physical world running in an unmaintained manner—like a merry-go-round that is never serviced. It is not a wheel that I want to or have to be on, and neither do you.

WE can be the change, because bottom line is that until that birthing into physicality we are all the same energetic essence—and of identical worth, alike wisdom, uniform capabilities, and the equal right to exist. We are all the same and choose to come for the same: to expand and calibrate as ONE.

We - women, men, and everything in between - need to get out of our forgetful fog and into our remembering ways to recall who we really ARE and how everything really IS. We need to rewind back to the basics and the beginning where:

Energy is all there is—and equality is all there is!

This highlights that you can certainly fight for the noble cause of equality and ask the same from others and the world, but until each one of us understands ourselves as energetically equal from the start, it will be the hardest and seem like an impossible job to do—all while our physical lifetime sifts through our hands like sand, possibly without us ever getting to the bottom of our personal purposes to experience our own happiness. At the end, equality in physical life is still battled, many desires are un-lived, and on it goes; this old and rusty merry-go-round.

However, if each one of us claims our natural equality and walks through life as such with a focus on seeing, feeling, hearing, thinking, expecting, and giving equality, the outpour of infectious-ness can be enormous—changing the world of physicality.

I say, show up as equal!

This does ask everyone to practice radical equality—for women, men, children, teenagers, white, black, albino, freckled, with scars or not, red hair or no hair, straight, lesbian, gay, bisexual, asexual, transgender, queer, old, young, poor, rich, dirty and stinky or clean and smelling wonderfully, laughing or angry, even offenders and prisoners, and followers of all religions. No exceptions!

Are you ready for that? I AM!

Be kind. Be smart. Be helpful. Be real. *Be a good person!*

WOMEN, FEMALES, AND FEMININITY

This is where we get to the bottom of it all. Not to worry though, we won't get all chicky about it…

FEMALE ENERGY VERSUS MASCULINE ENERGY

Not that this matters—but then again, does it?

As we covered above, we are all the exact same vibrational energy. Yet, you arrive in physical life as a physical woman and that carries different energetic information than being a man.

So yes, it does matter and you can use it to your advantage.

All energy carries information. For instance, take a cucumber that is energy just like you—yet the cucumber carries the information of juicy, green, to some earthy and slimy, to others fresh and cleansing.

What I am saying here, is that even though on the energetic basis we are all the same, once you arrive in this physical life as a woman you carry different energetic information than a man because of your physical form and your beautiful hips. Use them!

Sounds complicated? Well you are indeed a very complex clump of energetic information, but on the basic level you are very simple—energy, and one with all. The information behind your essence only becomes complicated when physically alive and not understood, but stays refreshingly simple and exciting when physically alive, understood, and living with the deep knowing of who you really are.

Let's dig in deeper:

Female or male energy in the physical realm does not mean one is strong and the other is not, one is beautiful and the other is not, one is gracious and the other is not. On the contrary, they both can bring the same information to light, it all depends as what type of woman or man you arrived here and further choose to be—small or big, tall or petite, gentle or aggressive…

All women and men have some of both - female and male - energetic information available as part of themselves with the ability to change in order to match one's preferences of living life—but one is typically many times more dominant than the other.

So, what is the difference then?

The energetic information of the physical body is definitely different—female breasts are sexy and motherly, nourishing with a gracious beauty that is felt in physical life form whereas a male's chest is more about muscular strength, also sexy, yet without nourishing information. The vagina carries the information of strong, embracing, spacious, safe, warm, and a place of protection. The penis is felt as strong, sexy, powerful, sometimes overtaking and in charge. Not to mention, the different hormones and juices that drive a female or male body and the capability of a woman to carry, grow, and give birth to a child—all different energetic values. Physically speaking, there are big differences, of which only these few were named.

On the mind level, the energetic information is that females are more connected, deeper loving, calmer in common sense, and more mature because of that, while men are more practically thinking, less emotional, and sometimes more superficially connected. This stems from ways that go far back in time and the upbringing of our ancestors because of these old beliefs, habits, and expectations. To this day, it is fact that girls are brought up with different values than boys—creating energetic information that are different in gender. Not for all individuals, but true for the masses.

On a soul level there is no difference, as we have already covered we are all neutral energetic beings. That is the same on the consciousness level—we are all the same energy, connected as one, constantly vibrating and sharing with each other.

Coming into this physical life, your energetic information immediately matters and is presented as you - a female or male - and then it is polarized through your upbringing, all while staying neutral on your basic energetic level. Later in life, many desire to learn how to neutralize back to the roots of a deeper connection to one's soul. A very natural wish, especially in the later phase of life or when concluding a life cycle. In reality, it is a wish to feel aligned with the energetic essence of who one IS and the one-ness with all of consciousness. Through all that you experienced in life, this will conclude into a more expanded and wholesome you—a purpose you came here for.

So whenever you are ready, mash it all together—both your female and male energetic information of who you are. From there, find the values that make you feel the happiest and make them the north star you want to be magnetized by and follow—to live your life as the woman that you ARE.

This is how I see it, for giggles... Once upon a time red and yellow potatoes were separate until a mad chef cooked them all together, then mashed them all together, into the most incredible yumminess there was. The whole village came to enjoy that mix-and-match and they all lived happily ever after, in absolute completeness, one-ness, and true wholeness. The End. Sounds like magic to me!

That's really all there is to the female and male energy: It's information that only matters on the physical life level and is in truth all made up, yet, is still really important for you to experience in your physical life. It's like the spice to your life that will give you incredible expansion to calibrate into what you are here for to BE.

And the cool part is that after a certain time of life experience, you have complete charge over it and can freely choose what your personal energetic information as your woman shall be. Carry that goddess vibe with pride and joy by NOT asking for equality but by claiming your unique-ity.

Be kind. Be smart. Be helpful. Be real. *Be a good person!*

WHY A WOMAN AND NOT A MAN?

Besides accepting that you did choose to come here as a woman - even if later in life you choose differently - and with that giving up comparing yourself to a man, have you ever asked yourself, "Why did I choose to come here as a woman? Why not as a man?"

This is a great question to ask yourself privately all the time, because I can guarantee that the answer is different in every phase of your life, and for every woman there is. It is also something wonderful to feel yourself into, as much as possible, in order to get closer to the bottom of why you are here right now.

And, it has nothing to do with men... So please don't get hung up about the "Why not as a man?" That's just for show purpose.

For example: In my phase of physical life right now - though in truth it was always like that - the answer and purpose is to really dig deep into the beauty and happiness of it all, into loving it all; into my ability of turning everything - no matter the nature - to be a gift, then sharing and spreading this goodness through my work with the world. It's like I spread butter on a piece of toast... Plentifully with excitement and great appetite. I'm European by birth and by heart, I love my butter.

As a woman, you hold infinite power to BE the mover and shaker through living your full female energetic essence without ever needing to feel in a lower and untruthful frequency. Lower and untrue in the sense of being a victim, comparing yourself to men, or any phrase that points out a physical equalization; "a woman can do the same as a man" or "girls can do that too."

For one, you are never a victim if you don't choose to live the victim energy. No matter what traumas you have experienced—explained deeper in the chapter **I am not a Victim—I Turned it all Around**. And two, you are *your* woman and not a man! There was never a comparison or equalization needed because I think that with the wisdom of this book and with the connection to your energetic essence you can do better than any un-connected man. And the men that are connected, they will pull and amplify your power with you.

It only makes sense that problems come into existence when you go against these two truths, by fighting against being a victim or showing up as a victim, and by trying to be like a man or trying to change men. I say, give up the fight to prove yourself worthy of a man and his capabilities because it creates a wrong sense of "there is an equality issue."

Plus since you can never live up to manhood - and why would you want to, since it's not better than womanhood? - it lowers you on the scale of worthiness without ever possibly succeeding. Just imagine a bird trying to live up to a fish… It makes me giggle, just thinking about it.

A better way to go about this is to radically and unapologetically BE and live the best ever as that incredible woman you came here to BE. From that powerful space - where equality already IS - you claim your throne and create the physical life changes that are long-lasting for you and every woman to come.

Back to the question, "Why a woman?"…

Look at where you stand in your physical life. Find the biggest physical life experiences that you have had in your past or are having right now. Highlight the ones that are because you are a woman—the ones that, as a man, you would not have had. Don't cheat by only choosing the good memories, but also dig up the bad, hurtful, and hard ones without getting emotionally involved or refreshing the feelings of pain. This is only for the purpose of making a list.

Here are my examples:

- I experienced sexual abuse, because I am here as woman/girl

- I was drugged by a man to unknowingly smuggle drugs, because I am a woman

- I was threatened in a relationship, because I am a woman

- I experienced being pregnant 3 times, because I am here as a woman

- I gave birth to 2 children, because I am a woman

- I miscarried a baby, because I am a woman

- I experienced breast feeding, because I am a woman

- I am a holistic practitioner, because I am a woman

- I am writing this book about being a woman, because I am a woman

- I love all beauty, happiness, and creativity as me, because I am a woman

Now, it is of absolute importance to me that you stop all compassion, empathy, or identifying yourself with my mentioned traumas immediately - if that is where you were heading - because not only am I not fishing for your heartfelt sympathy, it is of no value to you and me if you step into the lake of feeling them for me. If this puts the big question mark of "What's that all about?" on your forehead, I want you to jump to the chapter **Compassion and Empathy** *- yes, I wrote a whole chapter about these two very important feelings - with speed. There I explain how to feel those feelings in a good-feeling way—the only way, really. I promise, you will see that I am no cold-hearted woman because of what I just said.*

Take your list and add to each line what this physical life experience as a woman brought you—highlight *what* you experienced because you are your woman. This gives you clear reasons as to *why* you chose to come into this physical life as your woman.

Here are my examples:

Abused, threatened, drugged—spiritually, it taught me that I can feel good and be my pure positive energy even in and after these moments. By separating and then detaching my physical essence from my energetic essence, I realized that these types of oversteps only happened on my physical life level—in my energetic existence they don't matter. This is an empowering method for me and brings me further into my expansion of who I am—for my work I use it to get my physical self out of the way in order to connect with all the conscious knowing. There is more about this in the chapter **I am not a Victim—I Turned it all Around.**

Having children—well that is self explanatory… It is magic and heavenly wonderful to be a mom. My children taught me limitless things and to this day that is still the case. To learn more about my parenting adventures and style, check out my book **Parenting Through the Eyes of Lollipops**. I am also married to their dad, the love of my life, as my woman—best thing ever!

I am a holistic practitioner, healing-energy consultant, and a speaker because I am here as a woman. What does that mean for my work? I am able to use my female touch and my story as a woman to go very deep into feeling, sensing, and helping my clients, readers, and followers.

I am an author of three books. What does me being a female author have to do with that? Well, all my books are energetically charged with my female energy—helping and shifting many people, especially women, live better and deeper lives.

I love all beauty, happiness, and creativity—I don't think as a man I could experience life as beautifully as I am enjoying it as my woman, nor do I think that there is a man that could possibly feel what I feel. To learn more about my ways of living happily pick up a copy of **365 Days of Happiness: Because Happiness is a piece of cake**.

Now that you have your list of experiences and found all your glorious female reasons - and, hopefully, also celebrated them - moving forward you can immediately take the stand of "I AM a woman. I AM experiencing this because I AM my woman. And I carry my woman with pride and power" for every new experience to come.

I would even go further—intensify the reasons - not necessarily the feelings - of what you experienced or are experiencing because you are a woman, a million times more, then go BE and live them, because that is why you chose to come here as your woman. Express them fully by owning them!

This should answer your *why a woman*!

Be kind. Be smart. Be helpful. Be real. *Be a good person!*

DOES IT MATTER THAT YOU ARE A WOMAN?

Only to your physical you and only in your physical life realm!

That is where the only difference lies between a woman and a man—hence the woman has glorious mountain tops - two of them, mind you - and a female lotus flower surrounded by a gorgeous rose bush that many of us are depleting out of existence with shaving it all off. Not judging, just kidding! A man has none of those two said raised beauties, at least not to that extent. Of course there are some more physical body differences—hormones, muscles, and other juices.

Let's not forget the incredibly contrasting, many times conflicting, or often poles-apart type of minds, feelings, emotions, expectations, and likings that are matching up with the colorful palate of different capabilities between women and men—between the physically manifested versions of these humans that is. But don't get all worked up, nobody is ever smarter or more capable because of that, just different in physical essence.

Plus, there is the fact that your physical body carries a different energy by simply being either female or male—as we covered in the chapter **Female Energy Versus Masculine Energy**.

Non-physically, spiritually, soulfully, energetically, higher-powerly, and universal-conscious-lawfully, it does not matter in the least that you are a woman because there is no difference in that non-physical essence of what everything and everyone IS—energy!

To hold yourself energetically to the fact that you are a woman would not only be untruthful and impossible - since female and masculine differences are non-existent on the energetic level - but it would also undermine the true essence of who you are, all while pinching off your true and limitless energetic power that you have available at all times and that you actually always ARE.

Holding yourself on your physical life level to the fact that you are a woman with a female physical-energy, however, is incredibly powerful. And when the what, how, and why of your femininity is understood, you get the utmost usefulness out of that wisdom. I want to take it even as far as saying, "To get the most fun out of your life and to squeeze an unlimited amount of the most thrilling experiences for you to enjoy, until your last breath taken, you have to find a way to understand and shift that knowing into your natural way of BEing and living."

But that brings into the equation to claim your focused power of "being" that infinite, limitless, eternal, and energetic non-physical version of you—which exists in an open space of nothing-ness and consciousness where everything IS one and possible, first.

Secondly, realize the profound and elaborated knowing that you chose to come here as a woman—calculating the female energy that you are here as, that you are wanting to experience, and that you are so ready to calibrate and expand into.

When that is a rock-solid understanding and the natural connection between you and you, only then can you fully walk and show up as your most gracious female to rock the world. To vividly BE and live your "hotness"—your woman!

This brings forth the only truths there ARE:

• You are not here as a woman by mistake—even if you choose to change your gender later in life

• You are more than just your physical female body—you are an energetic non-physical essence first and foremost

• You are never powerless as your soul being—"no-power" only exists in the limited physical life form

• You have everything that you need available at all times—

on your energetic level

• You can understand, overcome, and find solutions for anything—on your soul level and in the space of consciousness

• Your deepest power lays in being your energy first and your physical essence second

So, does it matter that you are a woman?

Yes to be precise, you can make it matter immensely physically; how you show up in this physical world and how you choose to be while being here. Here it matters! That is where it starts and not an inch before—because before that, you are neutral energy, just like everything and everyone else.

Be kind. Be smart. Be helpful. Be real. *Be a good person!*

WHAT IS YOUR PURPOSE IN THIS PHYSICAL LIFE?

Your purpose - as it is for everyone else, even for men - is to truthfully BE your pure positive energetic essence—that is here as your perfectly chosen physical existence to live your unique physical life. A life in which you align with your personal happiness, joy, satisfaction, health, and success and dwell in the greatness of "I love my life, I love myself, and I love what I am doing!"

Nothing groundbreaking here, but so much good-feeling common sense.

Everything that IS in your life - the good, the bad, and the ugly - is meant for you to allow as an expansion and receive like it is the grandest gift ever. Pretend it is your birthday and unwrap it with delight, go ahead! Then, calibrate its meaning, and embrace the growth and heightening that just happened for you—the higher high-for-life frequency that you lifted yourself into because of it.

You have the capability to create your own physical life reality by thinking, feeling, and then vibrating in a certain frequency—all while physical life shows you where you stand by mirroring back to you how you are doing inside of your private you. Meaning, you can take charge of doing it all! I say, claim your complete creator-power by saying, "I take it! I own it!" or even "I did this!" to everything there IS—then unwrap the learning, enjoy the expansion, and off you go higher and higher. You are in charge!

For me, my experiences of abuse were some of those moments where later in life I learned to say, "I take it and own it!" because I was done with this intense hurting, with pushing it away, or wanting it gone. My mindset was set on "This is not defining who I am. I AM much bigger in energy than this physical life experience. I'll unwrap it. I'll expand with it. I'll calibrate into my highest essence because of it." I promised myself that from then on, "I am in charge!" and would make sure that my thoughts and feelings are aligned with a frequency that wouldn't allow this anymore. Moving forward in my life, I said, "I am doing it all!"

Now, it is of absolute importance to me that you stop all compassion, empathy, or identifying yourself with my mentioned traumas immediately - if that is where you were heading - because not only am I not fishing for your heartfelt sympathy, it is of no value to you and me if you step into the lake of feeling them for me. If this puts the big question mark of "What's that all about?" on your forehead, I want you to jump to the chapter **Compassion and Empathy** *- yes, I wrote a whole chapter about these two very important feelings - with speed. There I explain how to feel those feelings in a good-feeling way—the only way, really. I promise, you will see that I am no cold-hearted woman because of what I just said.*

And again, and again… I never endorse the physical life actions of abusers—owning it is all and only about becoming so selfishly self-centered and taking such unapologetic care of how I feel and think, in order to accomplish my full claim of my power over myself and my life.

In this process I became a master of creating myself and my life as I want it to be. As a wonderful side-effect, all my physical life experiences, the good, bad, and ugly received an invitation to shift to be neutral matter, energy, when desired. An environment in which I am able to look at everyone and everything freely, then sort what is mine and what has nothing to do with me. Sometimes I stare at it for days and days, to absorb the wisdom of what I, my life, and the world as a whole, is all about.

I draw a clear line about the *meaning* of being a woman and the *purpose* of a female essence being here:

The *meaning* is a state through which you shall experience your physical existence as your woman, in the sense of, "I am a woman, so what does it mean for me to experience this as my woman or because I am my woman?"

Through this meaningful insight, you live your *purpose* of being wholesomely yourself, your happiness, your health, your joy, and your success—which you then *purposely* share and spread with everyone and everything, to help *all* grow in this physical life, and expand in the energetic realm of consciousness.

The gigantic *purpose* of why you chose to come here is for you to be and feel the best and happiest, most joyous, healthy, and successful YOU possible, in order to make the energetic wheel go round and round.

This brings to light that in order to freely enjoy yourself in such a full way you must let go of all pressuring thoughts of how this amazing-ness has to show up for you. Instead, you need to practice alignment with feeling good, by being open, letting it all come in freely, and leaving it BE as fully as it IS.

It also asks for you to let go of any resistance that you might have towards yourself, anything, or anyone—by acknowledging all without judgment, and then accepting, respecting, appreciating, thanking, and loving the whole of what IS for you, for what it really IS—gifts! Some, clearly visible, and some in disguise, yet all are gifts.

Now you will want to look, find, create, and search for little baby-purposes here and there in your life. They will help you accomplish the main purpose of being happy, healthy, joyous, and successful along your physical journey. However, in the grand scheme of things it is never about the baby ones - sorry chocolate and red wine, it's not about you! - it's always about the gigantic, purely positive energetic one. At least, at the end of physical life IS where thinking and feeling this will be of satisfaction.

For giggles, try thinking about it like this; Life is like a soup with curry in it, but it's not about the curry. That spice is just a part of the bigger soup. Mind you, I love curry and could stand the curry on its own without the soup, but at the end of life I would not know about the soup—I would miss out on the nourishing, hunger-filling, and satisfying ways of that soup.

For me, that is a life not fully lived.

Happiness, health, joy, success, and all these high-for-life feelings, are energies that vibrate in the frequency of "your highest" purpose. They are feelings that are available for you to line up with what you are from the start, which is pure positive energy. Feeling them means you are BEing and living in the "highest of frequencies" of your purpose.

Guess what else is there? Everything wonderful that you always wanted, and all that you ever dreamt of. The life you really want to experience is in that frequency and if you are there too, you and your desires can meet and be together. You become one with each other and enjoy the purpose of flying even higher—since there is never a limit to how amazing you can feel and live.

More, better, and higher is a natural law of how physical life - and energy - IS. Just think of the last time you thought that "this is it" because you made it to the top of your feelings and experiences, when you caught yourself wanting something even bigger and better—and along came something bigger and better.

Your physicality is supposed to be like that! You as a whole being are supposed to be like that! Physical life - energy - is supposed to be like that! And in response to all those old beliefs and sayings of "It's never enough for you, you want too much, you are never satisfied, stop asking for more..." I say, nonsense! And if you are a parent that is battling this "more and more" with your kids, pick up a copy of **Parenting Through the Eyes of Lollipops**. I wrote a whole chapter about why it is such a wonderful frequency to latch onto.

I find this "always more and better" state immensely exhilarating and delightfully exciting to no end, and I see physical life to be phenomenally set up because of it—this next book exists because of "more and better" and because it's never enough.

Clearly your purpose IS to create and experience infinite

happiness for yourself through BEing and living the meaning of your woman you, while knowing that you are in charge of your gigantic energetic limitlessness.

Please - pretty pretty please - apply the urgency of, "It's my priority!" to this!

Be kind. Be smart. Be helpful. Be real. *Be a good person!*

WHY IN THE WORLD WOULD YOU COMPARE YOURSELF TO A MAN?

We women have evolved in who we are and what we want, yet even as expanded beings, many times we solve the problem of being freer and more accepted as women by practicing old ways of thinking and antique ways of empowering.

One way in particular is that we think that there is something wrong without separating that the only wrongness is on the physical life level. In order to change anything, we have to realize that on the energetic and consciousness level all is right - not wrong - and that the strength to change the physical lies in our strong connection to the energetic. It's like a toilet being clogged, yet we only swirl around the visible water - physical life - instead of reaching the pipes - energetic realm - through using a heavy duty plunger—our connection.

Another antique way is that we still look at our surroundings - men in particular - to solve what is wrong, when all along we can solve it ourselves by connecting with our limitless power. Change is first and foremost an inside job.

This brings me to our old expectations, at least subconsciously, for men to behave badly—hence the saying "That's typical men!"

Why is that so?

Because we are stuck - just like those rude men - and glued to the old belief that equality is nonexistent, and that we don't have all the power to make change happen—a power so strong, that it really does not matter what those masculine physical bodies are doing.

Again, I do not endorse abuse, this is all about becoming one with oneself.

Fact is, all change starts within—true for us females and

also for those men, but you get first dibs and the chance to have a speedy head-start by accepting that we keep the old merry-go-round going through our old beliefs, old recordings, and old expectations about ourselves, the world, and men in general. Once you claim that head-start in the speedy race of betterment, your momentum to vigorously step into your unlimited energetic power and cleanse, heal, renew, and create a "better" for yourself is a given.

That understanding and responsibility-taking starts a real and truthful female renaissance with a huge following—just watch all the wonderful men in the world applauding us and backing us. The truth is, one powerful light is always brighter than 1,000,000 unlit lights together - besides it being infectious - and light will always outshine the dark—that is on the physical level, because energetically, dark does not even exist.

Sure, in physical life it can be a real "anger management" pusher and go beyond your threshold when men still behave rudely, but really, is that what you base your power on—being a woman in physical life? And is that what you base your "power being taken away" on, men being rude or horrible?

My personal enlightenment when men behave rudely just because I am a woman, is that I am not in my power and not aligned with the force that I am. When this experience happens, and after I get my pretty energetic self to be the boss over my gorgeous physical self, I align with who I am soulfully—the result being that either this human-man doesn't bug me anymore, or the rude man turns into a big heart right in front of me. In truth, it's almost like I should thank him for serving me so well by being my physical-life ass-angel. Then again, that's up for debate…

As an example: When a man talks down to me I realize that I am showing up as my little girl, and as my little girl energy. Once I consciously shift back to being my adult woman I feel in my power again. Sharing THAT energy with him, he can let go of mirroring me what is so off in my alignment. Usually, this fixes everything. If not, I know that the rest is his and I leave it as that.

I was told by my hubby to explain the definition of "ass-angel," since that might not make complete sense to all. In my first book, **365 Days of Happiness**, I talked about ass-angels on Day 45. However, back then I was too chicken and ended up calling them "irritation-angels" instead. It makes me giggle to think how timid I was as an author. Today, and here, I am calling them what they are... Ass-angels!

In light of this we are all energy and the spiritual equivalent is angels. We are ALL angels, here to experience physical life. Yes, some are here to be your ass-angels, showing you how far off you are of your path of alignment. Others are here to verify that you are on point. Every angel - you too! - can be both, a dream-angel or an ass-angel—it really depends on how aligned one is. All I can say is, love ALL ass-angels, as they are serving as a compass for you. A wonderful purpose, if you ask me.

Every start can be hard, especially if you are hurt, and there is no guarantee that no more hurtful things will ever happen. But every change has to start somewhere, and it starts here— by taking full control, by not blaming others, and certainly by not waiting for change to happen.

I started to do so, and see clear evidence that my life and happenings changed from black to white, that the same hurtful happenings are not repeating themselves for me—and also not for my children. They grew up with this way of being, and the results clearly show in their progress.

You are so much more powerful when aligned with your energetic essence, and women are famous for being able to connect to their inner-self much deeper, faster, and easier, than men.

So use that! Never mind, if on a physical level, you are less strong when it comes to fighting. I am petite so I get it. If needed, I recall myself giving birth and how much power and strength I came up with, not to mention to then just turn around and say, "I'd do it again, and again, and again"—or how feisty I get when it's time to protect my children. We can put up a real good cat fight when needed. Shift into feeling this power!

Here is a great example: Equal pay!

Why are women demanding for equal pay by wanting to match men? Because in physicality men are earning more than women—at least in many jobs. A very limited demand though.

So think again when you say, "I want equal pay!" Equal to what, equal to being a man? That would not, and never will, give you justice because it implies an un-equality and a limit. Also realize the defending words you use to get your equal pay—that you as a woman can do just as good a job as a man. Those are old recordings, and if used, are keeping them alive. It's like being against all the plastic in the world while buying things that are still wrapped in plastic—every choice you make says either "yes" or "no" to how something is, and keeps going.

The best way is to not limit yourself ever! Instead, through your deep connection with the limitless energetic power that you are, expect that everything matches your own worth—even your pay. I can't wait to see what happens when you discuss your pay from *that* frequency.

Here is a great sequence of words that match a situation like that. Say, think, feel, and meditate on them often:

I know that men and women are all the same, only physically are we here as different. As that physical me I AM earning what I want, and I AM working as what I want. I have no need to compare myself to any man, or anyone else that is, because I am not a man, and I am not anyone else—I am not trying to be a man or anyone else. I AM my woman and came forth as such on my own willingness and in my own power.

I don't entertain the thought or conversation about

getting less than a man just because I am a woman. This is an untruth that sets me below—energetically and physically. I don't fight against getting paid less than a man or being valued as less than a man—those beliefs are not mine and never were mine. Instead, I am standing tall and proud as the woman that I AM, and fight for exactly that.

From my powerful energetic essence I AM changing everything! And so be it!

Breathe into the above and feel this plentifully.

You can literally shift any already lower-in-frequency existing situation and mold it to be a fit in your high-for-life frequency—if it's meant to be a match for your journey. If not, you will attract all "real" matches that are there for you, while vibrating in your high-for-life frequency. Meaning, you will get your perfect paying job after all.

Know that it's all in the practice of having a steady and clear way of being you—that is how you create your happy life. Be gentle with yourself, it takes practice. It does not take time though, once you are in, things will shift with speed.

Be kind. Be smart. Be helpful. Be real. *Be a good person!*

WHAT IT MEANS TO BE A WOMAN

To BE your own woman has different definitions for every woman. That's the beauty of it all!

Why you chose to come here as your woman in your physical female body, and why you focus on certain points of attractions in your physical life, are all ideas to look at. They make up great personal questions filled with profound value when asked in private and without any input of others. Explored every day or at a least often, while being in a meditative "nothing space," will give you the purest answers and results.

The motive behind finding yourself in your unique female meanings often is that life is an ever-changing and ever-moving energetic experience, meaning that your reasons and ways change too—with time, situations, and the maturity of your being. Don't be surprised if one main motive keeps popping up while others change to fit your constant new life situations, people, and life phases you find yourself in.

Let's set you up with a meditation - one that I mention in different variations throughout the book - for you to succeed in finding your female meanings:

Place yourself in a quiet room where you can BE and feel comfortable, safe, and open to whatever is coming in and up for you. Amp up the cozyness with candles, essential oils, pretty lights, and all things that light you into your glowing you—opening your female heart, your love portal!

Sit or lay, and cuddle yourself into a state of comfort to start breathing in and out deeply. Every breath in is welcoming your absolute relaxation into a wholesomeness of "nothing," and every breath out you let yourself go further and feel as you are floating deeper into that beautiful "nothing-ness."

When ready, ask the magical questions, "What does it mean for me to BE my woman right now, today, until I ask again?" "Why did I choose to come here as my physical female me?"

Let all inspirations, answers, visions, sounds, smells, and other forms of wisdom arrive freely. Welcome all of them, as each information is like a puzzle piece of your wholesomeness as your woman.

This wisdom is yours to feel, heal, and to shift into being your unquestioned knowing.

End this precious time with gratitude and love, and let yourself travel back into your now. Do this gently and with an unhurried agenda.

Breathe, and feel how you shifted as your woman into wholesomeness, knowing, enjoyment, and hopefully incredible excitement to trot down the street in your new day as your powerful female YOU! Time to get going, and move through your new NOW!

Practice this often and share it with other women—bringing great awareness to femininity and its momentum for women to rise.

Here is my experience in this:

Why I chose to come into this physical life as a woman and not as a man keeps me constantly on my toes. Crazy as it sounds, a lot of times I can't get enough of it and ask it uninterruptedly every split second, like a young child asking mom the same question over and over.

Why? It's fun, and keeps my always-bored and expansion-loving personality creative. I see this tuning-in as the grandest adventure to be on… I constantly learn about myself and can always shift to a better fitting way to BE myself. Besides, nobody ever gets to figure me out, because right when they get comfortable with who I am, I already asked again. Makes me giggle every single time.

In truth, I love flowing with the ever-changing and infinitely possible universal force that I am here to BE and live as. It's a constant new-ness that has endless potential to live my life to the fullest and most glorious plateau possible. The secret of living my best life lies in the ever-changing energetic essences, and not in the stagnant attachment of physicality, situations, things, and people.

My one gigantic reason that keeps coming up as a basis of what woman I am here to BE, is to point my focus on beauty, happiness, and creativity; in me, on me, as me, and around me. Sounds like three big reasons but if you know me, it's really three melted to be one—my very complex Jacqueline-reason. Some call it a handful one—to my delight. I consider that handful reason my main-squeeze that has shadowed me wherever I am going in my physical life as my physical female being. I see, feel, think, taste, smell, and hear beauty-happiness-creativity in a way that I could not if I would be here as a man. I live it purposefully through the essence of being my woman—through my feminine body, feminine mind, and feminine feelings and expectations; through my boobs, vagina, period, and my always "with lipstick" lips; through birthing my healthy kids and miscarrying one child; through my abuses, and through all other physical life experiences that I am creating for myself as I go… All things that me, as a man, could not do. That IS what it means to BE my woman!

I invite you to go on your constant woman-reason-finding adventure, and enjoy what you get out of it with ruthless embracement. So much so, that looking left or right at other women, at men as a whole, and silly rules that are only in physical life, have no significance whatsoever on your essence of your energetic soul magnitude of being your woman.

As a closing to this important chapter of **What it Means to BE a Woman** I want to highlight that it is high time for a feminine rising. However, it is not done through female physicality first—at least not with ease. It is done by claiming one's energetic limitless power first, that is then lived through and as that female physical human being—to fulfill its physical life purpose of living the best life ever.

Important! Not to be done with the purpose of rising above men. This is how women can and will rise. This is how the physical world can and will change—with ease and an ASAP-ness.

That's what it means to BE your woman!

Be kind. Be smart. Be helpful. Be real. *Be a good person!*

SHIFTING INTO FEMALE BLISS

Female bliss is the best—elegant, classy, majestic, queen-ish, and made of what creates worlds… Shall I go on, or are we in agreement that we must shift to that?

MEETING AND GREETING YOUR WOMAN

To get you calibrated and vibrating in the high-for-life frequency of feeling intuitively and automatically phenomenal about being you, a woman, and living your life as your woman, it is crucial to set the right stage.

Let's set you up with a meditation - one that I mention in different variations throughout the book - for you to succeed in meeting and greeting your woman:

Place yourself in a quiet room where you can BE and feel comfortable, safe, and open to whatever is coming in and up for you. Amp up the cozyness with candles, essential oils, pretty lights, and all things that light you into your glowing you—opening your female heart, your love portal!

Sit or lay, and cuddle yourself into a state of comfort to start breathing in and out deeply. Every breath in is welcoming your absolute relaxation into a wholesomeness of "nothing," and every breath out you let yourself go further and feel as you are floating deeper into that beautiful "nothing-ness."

Once you are in that blissful state, say, think, and feel the following:

I AM me!

- **I really, really, really like being ME!**

- **I really, really, really love being ME!**

I AM a woman!

- **I really, really, really like being a woman!**

- **I really, really, really love being my woman!**

I live my life as a woman!

- I really, really, really like living my life as a woman!

- I really, really, really love living my life as my woman!

Let all that you sense with these words unleash in you and for you, freely. Feel the difference and heightening in frequency between "I like..." and "I love..."

This wisdom is yours to feel, heal, and to shift into being your unquestioned knowing.

End this precious time with gratitude and love, and let yourself travel back into your now. Do this gently and with an unhurried agenda.

Breathe, and feel how you shifted as your woman into wholesomeness, knowing, enjoyment, and hopefully incredible excitement to trot down the street in your new day as your powerful female YOU! Time to get going, and move through your new NOW!

Best is to elaborate in this way of centering yourself as your woman every single day or at least as much as possible. Write your thoughts and your thoughtful shifts to BE closer to who you really are in a journal and enjoy that your writings change every single time. Not only are they an incredible written statement of your growth in your physical life story, they are also a sturdy way to put one building block onto another to build your own powerful house, mansion, or castle that is yours to BE and live in and as.

Who knows, someday you might like to stroll through those journals again with amusement, or for your children to read them in deep honor to get to know you on a complex spiritual level. Either way, they are a potent and well-deserved tool for you and nobody can ever take them away. You thought of them, felt them, and wrote them.

The joy of living extraordinarily in your inner quarters and looking out the window without a care in the world about what others are building, what others are trying to tell you to build, or what others see in what you are building, is your resultful way of living through playing with the above practice.

You will rise above everything and everyone with such a powerful light-speed tempo - leaving everything and everyone else in the dust - they won't even know where you went or what just happened. You will be out of their sight and out of their focused mind, a high-for-life state where minding what men and others do, can do, are able or capable of doing, are earning, or are privileged for, won't even be an option for you. You will be too busy enjoying your height!

This does not mean to settle for being quiet and accept wrongness in society. It means that whatever you are here to do as your woman you will accomplish from the most purest, happiest, healthiest, and most powerful way of being you.

For some that means you are an activist. Just think of the results you will achieve when demonstrating as that powerful you FOR the incredible essence of being a woman, versus from a weakened you against all that is wrong in the world.

For others that means being a home-stay mom—imagine the powerful results you have for your children and family. They will be saturated with your sureness, knowing, and wisdom to the point and outcome of raising over-the-top empowered humans.

Then there are the beautifiers, like me—when I am in my highest essence of me, my inspirations, actions, and results are world-moving, producing nothing else than pure joy for me and others, and glittery beauty while at it. My best work of helping people live better lives is created from there.

The bottom line is do whatever floats your boat, and your woman, from your purest and most potent infinite powerful space; guaranteeing the biggest impact on yourself and others while allowing you to receive exactly what you want, because you are vibrating in the frequency where what you want actually exists.

Know that in order to fly high, you have to choose to feel good first—only then can you create physical life actions that create your next and new high-for-life to BE.

Be kind. Be smart. Be helpful. Be real. *Be a good person!*

YOU OWN TWO APARTMENTS—DID YOU KNOW THAT?

I know that by now you are aware that you are energy and your whole being is made up of a physical body, mind, soul, and consciousness—nothing new.

In this chapter, I want you to think of yourself a little differently. It's a little silly, actually. Imagine that you are a whole house with two apartments, very comfortably walking step by step forward in the path of your wonderful life journey, one you came here to live and experience.

Are you excited yet? I am! I am very excited for you.

As that whole house, you possess the cool function of always being able to split into two parts of yourself—the physical apartment and the energetic apartment. It's always by choice, sometimes space is simply desired - or actually needed - to be and breathe alone either physically or energetically. For fun, you can make this ability a button that once pushed is an immediate, "*swoosh*, and separated you are!" Don't worry, it's just a split in your essence and not in personality. Two phenomenal parts of you—double the trouble.

In that separation, each part of you gets to go into quietness and experience life in and from their own quarters—the physical apartment and the energetic one.

I like to think of it as two siblings that make up the children-gang of a family. Most of the time it's all giggles and ice cream, and yet... When trouble arises or space is needed, separation is key for future clarity and understanding.

So...

Take a minute to close your eyes, while breathing and feeling into being your whole house - how does that feel? - then imagine splitting and being in each separate apartment with the fitting essence of yours. How does that feel?

Here it is, step by step:

• Imagine yourself being the whole house. Make it a mansion, castle, or houseboat—whatever floats your joy. Feel into the complexity of your *whole you* hanging out as such.

• Imagine your physical essence retiring into your physical apartment. Close the door and feel how sitting in your physicality feels for you.

• Imagine your energetic substance going into your energetic apartment. Close the door and feel how it feels for you to be spending some time in your soul space.

All three visualizations above have very different vibes to them because they are different environments—one being wholesome, one being physical, and the other being energetic. This also means that it is only natural that there are different viewpoints, experiences, and solutions available in each place. As to why that is really powerful, I'll explain further down…

Normally and on a usual day you are walking as your whole house and are experiencing life as easy peasy, living in a playful and light manner. I say normally because that is the expectation you had when you originally decided to come here—to live as a whole in easy-peasy-ness. However, you also knew that trouble eventually will show itself, making that the new "normally," at least for a while. This trouble arriving-and-existing fact was never scary for you. You decided to come here anyways, because you knew that you have this split-option always available.

You knew that if trouble - we'll leave the details to your imagination - arose, you could separate yourself into your physical and energetic essences.

You knew that if you let your split parts run into their chambers immediately, they could breathe, feel, and relax into what is going on—without being overrun by the intense feeling-cocktail that a life-happening initiated for you.

You also knew that by separating, you can collect yourself and steady yourself back to a better feeling you - one that can see, feel, hear, taste, smell, and think of what is happening from a good and fitting viewpoint - result being, you can resurface with a new-ness in solutions that otherwise would not be visible as your whole house.

Elaborating on it as a story, it would look something like this:

Your whole house is on the move in an easy-peasy-ness… But trouble appears! You say as your whole to your two essences, "Hey, there is trouble! I can see it, feel it, hear it, smell it, taste it, and my mind is thinking about it! Let's separate and get out of here!"—like a thief and his thief buddy robbing the jewelry store… If trouble makes an appearance, they get out of there and separate immediately!

From there it's pretty simple: feel yourself into your physical apartment—how does that stubborn trouble feel when looking through your physical eyes in your physical life? Is it solvable in physical life? Can you find a solution as your physical you? Is it hurting too much in physical life? Is this an adventure that you want to experience in that intensity, as your physical being?

If your answers and feelings are indicating that it's a no-go zone for you or that it does not feel good for you in your physicality, then it is time to shift yourself to BE and experience from your soul space—an oasis made of pure positive energy where nothing is ever wrong, but everything always IS neutral and fine; where all experiences are a great gift for expansion and calibration; where there is always a solution, and where there is plenty of space since it's the bigger apartment to BE and live in, hence it's the bigger part of you.

If physical life ever gets too much, too painful, or too troublesome, shift to BE and live solely in and as your soul space. Rest there! Through seeing with your soulful eyes, listening to your soulful guidance, enjoying your soul passion, and understanding your soul journey, you will find relief, strength, and healing in solutions that will aid you to stay true to yourself—solutions that to the naked physical eye are not always visible.

That is why your split-super-power is so valuable. You get to experience physical life and have a rest-way out, or healing-way through, that goes beyond your physical wisdom and into infinite possibilities. Like the basement of a house, that will protect you with its underground stability when a tornado hits.

Now you know why you never even thought twice about coming here—even though you knew that trouble was either waiting or jumping at you like the street guys hiding and jumping out to frighten people for fun. That, by the way, really is a thing—we were startled like that as tourists in San Francisco down by the pier. But like I said, no fright for you, only split!

You are the proud owner of two very beautifully fitting apartments. Furnish them to your liking! Don't neglect them by leaving them empty or forgetting to have sleepovers once in a while—to then walk as your whole house again, as your whole being.

Be kind. Be smart. Be helpful. Be real. *Be a good person!*

IF ALL YOU DO IS BREATHE, EAT, SLEEP, AND BE HAPPY...

… It's a good day!

As a whole being - a physical body, mind, soul, and consciousness - it is of utmost importance that you create a healthy environment in all of your components. Without this, it is very unlikely that you are centered in the middle of who you really are, and aligned with what you came here to BE and calibrate into.

Think of when you are exhausted or unhealthy and trying to see life as sweet and colorful—still possible, yet a hard starting point. This is a very truthful fact for everyone.

Feeling well means you have the natural capability to BE your power and show up as such—fun times indeed!

How do you take care of all your components?

For your physical body: It has very specific needs at different times and phases in your physical life. To find out what they are, have conversations with your body and ask what it needs—chat with your pain, your physical symptoms, and your physical disharmonies. Follow the answers and instructions with determination and your deepest self-love. Some obvious needs are lots of sleep, plenty of water, fitting movement, and clean food for nourishment; some higher frequency ones are hobbies, meditation, massages, laughter, gratitude, appreciation, and humor—for me and still to this day, chocolate and red wine have very high-for-life qualities.

For your mind: Acknowledge all of your thoughts as fine ones—none are good, none are bad, they just are. Stay judgement-free! Accept, respect, appreciate, thank, and love all your incredible thinking as part of you. Then notice the thoughts that are not aiding you and don't make you feel good, shift them to better-feeling ones. For instance, from "not enough" to "plenty and abundant" or from "ugly" to "beautiful." Practicing this often makes positive thinking your normal way of living.

For your Soul: Your Soul is the truth of who you really are—an energetic essence with limitless soul-wisdom you can draw from. Your heart hosts your soul, so it only makes sense to focus on nourishing your heart through creating and experiencing heart-touching moments. Consciously feeling these happy times aligns you with who you really are - pure positive energy - and fills every single cell of your whole being with infinite well-being—happiness guaranteed. Make heart-soul nourishment a daily priority!

And for your consciousness: Your consciousness is your energetic one-ness in your NOW! Focus on what is going right for you in your NOW. This can be your breath giving you life, your feet running after your kids, your job bringing you money, your loved ones, the sun and moon showing up, or anything that is going right for you. If needed, use the help of a mental microscope to find the smallest going-right-particle, because good is always there for you. Stop talking about what is going wrong! That stops the focus and momentum of the unwanted, giving the wanted a chance to BE. Instead say, "It always works out for me, for you, and for us!" which supports you in being and living with a positive attitude as one with your consciousness.

Creating a healthy environment in all of your being's components is an inspiring demonstration of well-being for yourself and anyone that sees you. It offers a solid foundation that cannot be shaken by anything or anyone because you create it for yourself. It's your way in which you say the "how, when, where, and what"—always ready for you to feel and breathe into it. You own it!

As such a wholesome entity you find all the strength you need to radically stay true to yourself and breathe freely—and by all means, if your truth as that super-healthy glob is to run split naked around the block once, twice, or thrice… Go for it, just don't tag me in your pictures saying I told you to do so...

The value in this picture is that no matter what you are truly wishing to do or BE, you will be able to do it in such regal graciousness and will look so natural while doing your "meant to do" thing that nobody can or will ever question you. And if they dare, you won't care.

It's like that friend who got new glasses, a new piercing, or a new tattoo and all you can say is, "It looks like you always had it." The explanation here is that they were 100% aligned with themselves when they chose the "new" and are 100% aligned with the "new" being part of their wholeness. A meant-to-be match made in heaven!

Taking amazing care of your whole being makes it possible for you to feel incredible, and BE and live yourself from a pure space of clarity and knowing. Your choices will be fitting and aligned with who you are—as one.

Important! It is never too late for you to start connecting with your whole being and to make positive, healthy, and happy your normal way of living. However the earlier you start, of course, the better.

And... Why would you wait for better times to walk your journey in the most freeing and high-for-life way, anyways?

Be kind. Be smart. Be helpful. Be real. *Be a good person!*

ACTIVATE YOURSELF...

...Physically, mind-mentally, soulfully, and consciously!

What do I mean with that?

An activation means to turn something on and make it go—this action is of a very empowering nature. Try it! Say, think, and feel: "I AM activating myself on every level!" Breathe into the empowerment of this strong sentence.

By being a physical body, mind, soul, and consciousness, you are a complex being and as such you want to operate when being fully activated—firing on all cylinders. This makes a lot of sense, since as a whole, you have the most power through which you can experience vividly, enjoy the most energy, and hear the deepest wisdom—it's easy to feel wonderful as your physical skin in this physical realm.

A great question that I love to ask myself often, is "Which part am I living mostly from right now?" This answers whether I am dominantly oriented to experience things physically, mentally, soulfully, or from my consciousness.

Many times I catch myself fully living from where I am mostly comfortable, the energetic essence. While being a holistic practitioner working with and in energy, consciousness, and the quantum it is a fabulous choice, when dealing with bills, housework, or driving it proves to be a less worthy and trusted one. There, a balance is what I pull myself into—evenness between physical, mental, soul, and consciousness. Otherwise I would keep floating like a balloon, full of bliss, lightness, and wisdom somewhere in the untouchable sphere. Sounds like fun until cars behind you start honking their horns because you are an energy-dreamer and as such are standing still with your car. Fun fact here, is that when they are yelling, "Put the darn phone down!" I am saying in delight, "What phone?!?"

A full soul without the physical shell being active is a great way of explaining my energetic over-activation here—accident prone indeed. My bruises can fill a whole book.

My family is a great help to even me out because they want food, a clean house, an unclogged toilet, and to be driven somewhere. At first I always go, "but... but... but..." because I am real cozy in my energetic realm. However, since their needs always win, and should, I get to remember that I am here to experience the physical vividly and enjoy real physical life happenings, problems, and joys. Thanks guys!

Being physically over-the-top means you are having trouble hearing your inner voice, don't feel a connection to your soul being, and it's hard or impossible for you to sense your energetic essence. You reason only with what you can see, feel, think, hear, smell, taste, and touch in front of you with your physical body and in your physical life. As an example, if I tell you that money is on the way, that it's already here for you in energetic essence, you wouldn't believe it until you see it. This makes you a physical life realist without using the power of the energetic soul-essence—making it pretty limitless, and somewhat powerless.

As the mind over-bearing one—you think, think, and think some more. You can't stop it and are always thinking things through. You don't necessarily have to see it manifested, but you have to think it, otherwise you can't make sense of anything or anyone. Your mind is tricking you into thinking that you don't have to feel it, instead only think it. A thought-rollercoaster ride indeed—one that is faking its realness!

The consciousness-crazy one is always feeling one with all—those around and all of consciousness. Which sounds amazing until you realize that you have no personal priorities physically, mentally, or soulfully. You are one with all and have no own physical shell in that one-ness. This could be a world helper that gives up oneself completely with the sole focus to save the world. Not only is their personal life-purpose forgotten, but these actions are also silly when the universe clearly states that there is nothing that needs to be saved—only aligned.

As you can see, any strong side-taking brings an imbalance into your being of wholeness. A sadness or unwell-ness is naturally felt because parts that are yours to experience as this physical you in this physical life are not used and lived. Some might not even be activated. It's like renting a whole palace with many rooms but only stepping foot into the tiniest room—while the electricity in all unused was never activated. An unexplored adventure, if you ask me.

It is important to activate, awaken, and use the parts that are a bit forgotten, uncomfortable, or maybe even un-cozy for you. However, first you need to know of these parts and find out what your most used and lived one is—from there you can make a plan on how to get the others fired up to 100% too. Balance created!

In the imagination of that palace, you would turn on all electricity and start running and dancing through all rooms, parts, corners and nooks, in order to live the experience of that palace fully and vividly.

I say activate! Or why else did you rent your grand place— your whole being? Why else did you choose to come here as this wonderful whole being capable of living the best life ever?

Here are ways to activate:

For the physical: Take great care of your physical needs. Exercise, travel, enjoy feeling therapies such as massages, sexual pleasures, and other feeling opportunities: indulge in extreme adventures, like jumping out of an airplane like I did many years ago, or hiking to the top of a mountain. Love your physicality!

For the mind: Think, think, think—positive would be best here. Focus on mind games and mind puzzles that shift negative thoughts to positive ones. Do mind gymnastics, day-dream about your perfect life, imagine yourself flying a dragon... Use your mind until you can't think anymore, until your brain hurts. Love your mind!

For the soul: No need to activate your soul because this bigger part of you is always ready when you are... Connecting is the action here, by nourishing it with listening, feeling, sensing, and asking questions then hearing the deep wisdom that comes in and up as your customization. Follow your knowing with diligence, play with this, and feel your energetic essence. Fall in love with your soul!

And for consciousness: Feel yourself, while laying down, connected, shared, and one with all—without the outline of your physical body as a present feeling. That IS your consciousness. This one-ness is radical and not directed by life or other's behavior. All is one; the good, the bad, and the ugly—a space where you have enough neutral love for all and life as a whole. Love your consciousness!

When you are activated as a whole being, you can walk through life in a deliberately created balance. Sometimes this means that parts of you are more active than others—while it also can mean that you are in complete and balanced equality. The fun part is that you always have everything you need handy—a healthy way of flowing with all of life to the exact point you promised yourself you would, when chosen to enter this physical time.

In the picture of the palace, when every room is activated, you can walk through that palace in a deliberately created balance by always having everything you need handy—a fun way of flowing with the fact that you live in a palace. Way to go!

What are you waiting for? Activate! It's going to be an insanely active, yet balanced, ride.

Be kind. Be smart. Be helpful. Be real. *Be a good person!*

IMPORTANT LOOSE ENDS

Those pesky loose ends, never know where to put them, yet, they are so needed...

WHERE DOES YOUR POWER LAY?

Your weakness lies in measuring yourself against men on the physical-body and physical-life level by wanting the value of physical equality, by wanting the same physical life experiences, or by trying to change men all together.

Those actions are digging around the symptom, because physicality is symptomatic as well as being limited. It's like having a headache and treating it with painkillers - that are limited - when all along what you needed was to drink water. The headache will re-surface again and again until you treat the root-cause, your dehydration—a clear dis-aligned disaster because either you are constantly extinguishing symptoms or are not digging as deep as you could, which means you are leading an exhausting life not fully or vividly lived. Not to mention, that the relief is only "short-lasting" and that you are giving up your power.

Take coffee and tea, both are energy because that is all there IS, yet both manifested in this physical world as different beverages with very different tastes, purposes, and diverse experiences they share with us. They both are existing right next to each other in this physical paradise. They leave each other alone to shine in their purposeful power, their bright light. The coffee is not asking the tea to move aside, to change, to be different, or to be respected more and vice versa. They lack the desire to try to be like the other or ask for physical life equality, and for giggles, just think how it would be—you ordering coffee that tastes like tea. They simply are here in their full power to BE and taste as themselves—a powerful way to succeed.

So where does your power lay?

In living up to your complete and absolute energetic power - which is the same, and unlimited, for women and men - and aligning this with your physical female body to live a woman-oriented life—THAT is infinitely powerful! Gives me excited goose bumps just thinking, writing, and reading about how deep you will dig this way and how high you will fly because of it.

In other words:

Your energetic essence aligned with the female energy - more about that in the chapter **Female Energy Versus Masculine Energy** - of your physical body, then living and experiencing your female life from and through that energetic super-power—that is the complete shizzle.

As that power your thoughts and your focus are deliberately and solely pointed at you, making your energetic essence and physical appearance gigantic. There you can do whatever you want without men needing to hear you, see you, respect you, treat you better, step down, or move aside for you, because where men stand and what men are doing - wrong or just generally - won't be important in your gigantic-ness. This is where your power lies!

To me, my energetic power always was and IS available— back in time and still to this day. I know that it is always there for me to align with in order to gain incredible healing and expanding momentum in every single moment of my life. I felt this fact back when I was little and I know it with surety now—no matter what happens on my physical life level.

Of course, that does not give men the freedom to do wrong or overstep. I never endorse any form of abuse, no matter the age or gender. It is never OK and is in serious need of attention, complete believing of the victim, limitless understanding and support for the hurt, and the absolute accountability of the abuser—always aligned with the victim's wishes.

Under the surface - energetically - women and men are here as the same but manifested into physicality with different ways, causes, and purposes. Both women and men can live with this understanding right next to each other without needing one to change, or BE and experience like the other. Take trees… They are here as trees drawing from the source of their energy, feeding each other, yet every tree is present with a different look, smell, growth cycle, and purpose—through the same energy but as different trees. Women and men are no different.

You are not here as a physical female body that is drawing from the limited power of its physicality and trying to live or grow an inner being—that way has "victimization" written all over.

You are here as your energetic soul essence, furnished with the perfect soul power to draw from, and through that you live your life and purpose as a woman—whatever that might look like. This is sheer power!

Be kind. Be smart. Be helpful. Be real. *Be a good person!*

I AM NOT A VICTIM—I TURNED IT ALL AROUND

This dear-to-my-heart chapter is the result of me being sneaky so I can explain the spiritual and physical meaning of overstepped actions towards women, or really anyone—at least what I gathered, for myself, from this curious adventure called life.

If this happened to you too, then you will gain absolute strength by reading this. If it never happened to you but you know a woman who had this experience, this will give you strength to support that woman, and if you have a daughter my words will give you a backbone to talk about the sensitive subject of abusive physical life situations. Regardless, I think you should read it no matter your situation!

When an overstepping occurs, and for living a blissful life in general, it is very important to realize that your life has two components; a physical life one and an energetic one. You are living this physical life as, and experiencing it through, your physical body, but first and foremost you ARE an energetic essence—some call it a soul being, a spiritual being, your inner being, your highest good, whatever resonates with you.

What does that mean for an overstepping?

The sexual and emotional overstepping in my life happened when I was a little girl, and again later in my 20's. To get really general here, in cases like that there is an abuser and a victim— on the physical life level both are clearly very different. However, on the energetic level, me and my abusers were both the same—two energetic essences outfitted with a physical body, a mind, a soul essence, a soul guidance, a soul passion, and a soul purpose living our soul journey in this physical life.

Now, it is of absolute importance to me that you stop all compassion, empathy, or identifying yourself with my mentioned traumas immediately -

if that is where you were heading - because not only am I not fishing for your heartfelt sympathy, it is of no value to you and me if you step into the lake of feeling them for me. If this puts the big question mark of "What's that all about?" on your forehead, I want you to jump to the chapter **Compassion and Empathy** *- yes, I wrote a whole chapter about these two very important feelings - with speed. There I explain how to feel those feelings in a good-feeling way—the only way, really. I promise, you will see that I am no cold-hearted woman because of what I just said.*

So on we go…

Does that make the abuses OK? No! Never, and I will never condone any of it.

Did I wish on my physical life level for this to happen to me? No, of course not! Nobody ever wishes for that. But I chose to come here to experience my physical life to expand in my soul essence, and it just so happened that early on it started out with these hurtful physical life abusive experiences that, in reality, had nothing to do with me.

Did I hate my abusers or was I mad at people for not protecting me? Yes, of course! That anger and hate were important feelings for me to feel on my physical life level, in order to expand energetically as my soul being.

As physical life experiences - some hurtful and some phenomenal - happen and living this life as me is what I came here to be involved in and expand into, I decided early on to get to the bottom of what life really means for me.

I came to the well-feeling conclusion that I want to BE and live my life fully and vividly and as a deeply connected soul that enjoys this physical time on earth immensely. I figured out that this can only happen as soul-equals with everyone, no matter if they're here as a good or bad physical being, and no matter if they are hurting me or not.

The most healing occurrence was that besides me stepping into my complete power by promising myself to BE and live my complete soul essence, I realized that I have the function to separate my energetic me and my physical whole - my physical body and my physical life - from each other.

In that function I consciously was able to choose to become two essences - please read more on this in the chapter **You Own Two Apartments—Did You Know That?** - so that I was able to look at what happened to me from both my energetic, and my physical, essences.

I knew that this would create different viewpoints, holding different learnings and different healing methods for me. My thought and expectation was that one might be more helpful to me than the other in this hurtful time, that one can solve it for me by bringing me further in my expansion of energy and life, whereas the other would keep me deeply hurt and stuck in this trauma.

I deliberately decided to love myself enough and chose to focus on the one essence that helps me heal. In case someone was wondering, I have never lived in denial because of it. I simply chose to be bigger than the experience and then used it to grow. I used to call this process, "creating a happy bubble for myself."

In that separation and eventually in siding with my soul being, I was able to recognize that these oversteppings had nothing to do with me and that "losing my power" only happened on my physical level - physical body and physical life - without me ever losing my power on my energetic level.

It also let me, at least partly, think of my abusers as soul beings too—which helped me in the sense of not thinking of them as physical beings, because there they were the most disgusting human beings ever. It gave me relief.

This separation also let me understand the energetic value of these traumatic physical life events, so that I could use them to expand into the millions of growth possibilities that were there for me to calibrate myself into. This gave me healing and purpose.

Another one of my glorious examples, is that it took until I was about 16 years old for my red hair to start making sense to me, and others, in a time in Europe when having red hair still meant that you are a witch for many. Until then it was a real challenge to be alive as me in my physical life because I was alone and bullied—I felt unloved. The bullying, hurtful teasing, and mostly alone-time, made me think about happiness so much that once again I separated and created my own happiness bubble to BE and live in—a space where my red hair was OK.

Funny enough this became one of my biggest strengths ever, because to this day I take full responsibility for making myself happy. I am a very independent happiness-er by knowing how to be happy anywhere at anytime—all by myself and despite my circumstances. To understand my happiness process, I urge you to pick up a copy of my book **365 Days of Happiness.**

At some point I stopped hating my red hair while being outside of my bubble, and instead I started to love it—the side effect being that others stopped bullying me instantly. They started to respect my red glowing hair that they had called "night-stand lamp" for the longest time. My point is, that once I shifted into my power and changed my attitude, my surroundings shifted too.

Also, these painful feelings of being alone, sad, and angry were important for me to feel on the physical life level, a crucial experience that calibrated me to my widest and most potent expansion on my soul level—all while helping me realize that on the soul level those bullies and me were always the same, just soul essences here to live our physical lives.

Again… Is this OK? No! Never!

But if you decide to soulfully embrace what happens on your physical life level, you will make sure that you live your potent power of being a woman with pride and strength and ensure that, moving forward, you never create for yourself in the future what has happened for you in your past.

The exhausting fighting motion of "I want it to go away" will move aside for the permission for "it" to stay as a physical life experience, enhancing your expansion on your soul level. "It" becomes part of you, and grounds itself into your roots of who you are for the rest of your physical life—becoming the important ingredient of power and strength for you to know what you don't want, with that, knowledge of what you do want, the result being you are creating what you want with diligent force and incredible laser-like focus.

I knew then - and I know even more now - that by standing strong in this way of living, I can expand the most, live my unique power fully, and take right of the control to create my own life experience through the know-how of what happened. I see it as rolling out my own red carpet, as I go, from the purest source of who I AM.

Believe me; living this way, nobody will want to mess with you anymore—just as nobody wants to mess with me anymore. And if they ever try to mess with me, I know that I am not doing the powerful work of "embracing what was." I am not letting it root deeply inside of me.

Simply put, I am not showing up as the absolute power that I AM, which leads me to shift myself back to *who* I really AM. Freshly rooted and all dressed up in my warrior energy, nobody will mess with me but instead only give way to my presence.

I personally prefer to focus only a teensy bit on what was - especially the horrible what was - and more mightily on what I want my *next* to BE. This is my action of power that I step into and share—this holds me steady in my control of what I want to create as my furthermore, since we create our *next* with what we are saying, thinking, and feeling right now.

I think with my history, and as a woman, I have earned the right - if there is ever anything to earn, anyway - to say that it really does not matter what traumatic events happened in my past.

Instead, what matters is that I can say with absolute surety that I turned what happened into an even more powerful meaning of, "I am not a victim because I turned it all around." I hope that this can be your truth too!

Be kind. Be smart. Be helpful. Be real. *Be a good person!*

YOUR TRAUMA HIGHLIGHTS WHAT, EXACTLY?

Traumas are the flavor that everyone gets to taste, and they belong to physical life. Even your biggest enemy experiences traumas. We women are not special, or selected as the one and only ones, to call them part of our lives. So you might as well make your traumas your partner in crime and rob the jewelry store successfully.

Now that was just a metaphor—don't go rob anything, don't get in trouble, and don't waste your one call from jail on me. I'm busy, I have my next book to write.

All giggles aside…

I found that when I looked back at my biggest trauma and realized what this experience took away from me - or, rather, initiated a sickening malnourishment - it is exactly that energetic value of the "gone missing" that I am in need of in order to thrive.

I also found that even though I have plenty of the "missing" now, many times I can't really enjoy or live it. That is because I sabotage it with my old thought-and-feeling process I racked up during my old trauma. Since I never really had the "missing," I also never got to practice enjoying it, let alone get used to the good-feeling of it or pay attention to what it really means to have it. It's like being an unpracticed driver with a real driver's license—imagine that naïveté in very heavy traffic. Might as well leave the sign "please be patient—student driver" on the car for safety.

My biggest traumas of sexual abuse really robbed me of freedom—which was banished by someone else taking their freedom to their highest level by taking my freedom away from me. I was not asked for my opinion, never given the choice if I wanted things to happen, and I was certainly never presented with the fact that their doing stomps my freedom to the ground into nothing-ness. All my freedom was gone. A freedom-less being, indeed!

Now, it is of absolute importance to me that you stop all compassion, empathy, or identifying yourself with my mentioned traumas immediately - if that is where you were heading - because not only am I not fishing for your heartfelt sympathy, it is of no value to you and me if you step into the lake of feeling them for me. If this puts the big question mark of "What's that all about?" on your forehead, I want you to jump to the chapter **Compassion and Empathy** *- yes, I wrote a whole chapter about these two very important feelings - with speed. There I explain how to feel those feelings in a good-feeling way—the only way, really. I promise, you will see that I am no cold-hearted woman because of what I just said.*

On we go…

Since a long time now, I have had all the freedom in the world; freedom to speak, laugh, play, eat what I want, do whatever I want, and I have even been able to exercise freedom in my work—to write book after book, just as I please. Yet, I constantly felt that I am "not free" and that I have no freedom. Makes sense, since my freedom was taken from me a long time ago… No, it actually doesn't! Because now I am free and I have all the freedom in the world! So what in the whoops-a-daisy is so upside-down here?

I recreated - anew and anew - freedom-killing reasons, thoughts, and feelings that were all still driven by my old habits, beliefs, and old robotic programming of "I am not free!" that were created a million eons ago through my traumas.

Feeling so un-free in such a free life situation, meant that I am subconsciously operating like I have no freedom—but not because I did not have freedom, which is a huge difference! I sabotaged what I actually had and cultivated it back into the "missing, gone, taken away from me, not there" frequency, while feeling that people, the situation, the world, or life itself is still stripping me of my freedom. Realizing this made me think that I am going mad, while also knowing that this was a healing high-for-life "peekaboo" moment for me.

So with a skip in my step, I decided to fully and vividly embrace this newfound revelation of being a free being, and really learn how to enjoy it and let it fulfill me without any old memories of "no freedom" coming into the new and pure mixture of me.

This tactic of really looking at my traumas - old and new - and at what they robbed me of, then shining the spotlight onto the "missing" while consciously realizing that I actually do have this now in my life - many times in overflow mind you - made me understand myself better. I became complete—puzzle piece by puzzle piece.

To get you to puzzle together your pieces of completeness, ask yourself:

"What is my biggest trauma?" Don't relive or re-feel it— stay unemotional and stick with only remembering the happening.

"What is the one thing that this traumatic event robbed me of, or has taken away from me?" Again, don't dig deep into experiencing it—only realize what that "missing" was.

Shine a spotlight on it! Spend some time to really look at the missing piece by realizing that this IS what makes you "shine" today, and how you thrive in your NOW!

Then, ask yourself "Where in my life right now do I have this missing piece?" Small or big amounts, all count.

Consciously become aware of how much you already have it present in your NOW. Realize how you sabotage it with your old habits by putting it into your "missing" bucket again.

Important! Remember, nothing is wrong here, this is simply an acknowledgement that it is "high time" for this to be out and about and in your face, your spotlight.

Keep asking yourself "How can I enjoy and live my not even "missing" piece with new thoughts, fresh feelings, and fitting actions—for me to shine and thrive right NOW?"

Lastly, but never forgotten: "How can I create more of this goodness?"

Create your trauma story with every old and ancient trauma and also every new trauma or little heart ache that comes your way, moving forward. Promise—you'll catch up to your completeness so fast, that not being complete has no more space in your next, and next, and next, you complete being you!

This process has enabled me to start loving my traumas for what they are, a spectacular course on learning who I am in my experience of physical life. I love imagining them all being in my wonderful backpack that I carry with pride while walking my journey—meaning, I always have everything that I need in order to thrive even more, as me.

This makes everything a matter of "I don't care and love it all—because all of this is me!" Which is very powerful indeed.

I truly hope that you can fall in love with your beautiful and wonderful backpack too!

Be kind. Be smart. Be helpful. Be real. *Be a good person!*

WHAT ENERGY ARE YOU?

Aside from everything and everyone being the same energy on the most simplest level, coming into physicality as female or male and carrying a certain energy - as explained in the chapter **Female Energy Versus Masculine Energy** - there are also the four energies that the physical world is made of spiritually speaking:

Water, Earth, Fire, and Air.

Everything and everyone has all of these energies available to BE and live fully as their whole being with one always as the dominant one in this four-energy-constellation, shifting the others to be of a supporting nature.

However, the domination "throne-taking" changes through a lifetime—just as situations, people, and happenings change too. Whatever dominant energy one is carrying, is the energetic value said person is best capable of offering and teaching to the whole world at that particular time.

The fact is, that everyone is infinitely valuable, everyone has something to teach, and everyone has something to learn—which brings about a phenomenal co-creation throughout the whole world.

Understanding these energies invites you to look at the gifts of people - including yourself -carrying them in unique ways and in their unique journeys. You will find, that what often looks like limits or holdbacks, are indeed catalysts of greatness for the one living them.

The explanations of these energies and their polarities are:

Water: Denser in movement, flowing, peaceful, harmonious, yet always finding a way—think of a body of water like a wide river that is naturally flowing or a water fountain; flowing, clear, and dense water. A water-dominant person is a denser moving and deeper feeling person that often is living at a slower pace. It's a deeply and harmoniously grounded energy—wonderful to have present since life is a very fast-paced entity. Celebrate that energetic value, the peace and rest that the water energy brings, and the constant reminder of peaceful sanity. This energy is saint-like.

Earth: Mountainous, strong, unshakable, "I got this, we got this!"—think of a bold mountain that is steady and solid. A mostly earth person is a strong, steady, and grounding force that is keeping it all together and that you can lean on, like a mountain. This energetic value brings forth a "focused on the physical aspect of life" way. Welcome that energy as a grounded and safe feeling. Lean on this, it can hold you!

Fire: Fiery, moving fast, shaking things up—think of how infectious and fast moving fire can be and how it completely changes everything, once it passes through. This is a fast-paced person who likes to "stay on the surface" and keeps everyone - including themselves - on their toes, creating a speedy evolution and expansion while also teaching that it is OK to stay "on the surface" about physical life things and to not fall deeply into unwell feelings—not every physical life happening needs to be dissected at all times. This energy screams "Movers and shakers," and "Let's go people—right now!"

Air: Fun, light-ness, jolly, airy… Think of how the birds joyously fly through the air. That feeling is the energetic value of this element. Being light, bubbly, and mostly high-for-life wild, is the being that we are talking about here. When dominant they are either all the way up high or all the way down low—with the ability to bounce around in a split second. Having fun and being happy is the energetic value in this. Embrace the sunshine this energy brings.

It is also of immense value when you understand *who* is *what* energy in a family. Finding out the energy of each loved one and understanding their individual energetic value - and what they can offer and teach - is important for a harmonious family life because it shifts everyone, no matter how different, to be a phenomenal part of the pack. More on this in my book **Parenting Through the Eyes of Lollipops**.

Be kind. Be smart. Be helpful. Be real. *Be a good person!*

DOES YOUR LOVE WANT TO SPREAD OR NOT?

Love IS energy! It can spread in many ways—some leading you into connected-ness with your soul being, whereas others point you straight into disconnected-ness with your soul being.

In a perfect world you have enough love; so much so, that it overspills and that which is overflowing is up for grabs for whomever wants it, needs it, or simply just takes it. This grabbing effect has no input on you because you are still filled to the brim with your love while your healthy heart produces more as we speak. That IS a pure connected state!

However, the perfect world also includes times when you struggle with keeping your love cup filled, and forget about over-spilling. That is when your love does not want to spread, and spreading it anyways will send you into your disconnected-ness. It is usually your mind and thoughts that disagree with the non-sharing truth—all because of old recordings, beliefs, and habits of, "it's the good girl thing to do," the result being, you will run very low or even empty in energy, creating all sorts of distress while at it.

Taking care of your heart and your love and making sure that you are not wasteful with its created gold - or inviting gunk into the equation - is of the utmost importance, no matter the "what, who, or how" you are touching base with.

When my limiting old-self gets ahold of me and I need to find the "what, who, and how" that is best for me in order to reconnect with myself again, I use the following meditation practice, one that I mention in different variations throughout the book.

Here it goes:

Place yourself in a quiet room where you can BE and feel comfortable, safe, and open to whatever is coming in

and up for you. Amp up the cozyness with candles, essential oils, pretty lights, and all things that light you into your glowing you—opening your female heart, your love portal!

Sit or lay, and cuddle yourself into a state of comfort to start breathing in and out deeply. Every breath in is welcoming your absolute relaxation into a wholesomeness of "nothing," and every breath out you let yourself go further and feel as you are floating deeper into that beautiful "nothing-ness."

Once you are in that blissful state, focus on feeling your heart space and your powerful love as a whole. This can be a warm feeling, butterflies going wild, or a gentle nothing-ness that feels lovely. It is unique to you, and completely normal for it to change all the time—sometimes even while the meditation is flowing. Breathe into that.

After a little while, feel only the essence of your love—an energy of power, denseness, and solidness. Motherly at times. Breathe into that.

When ready, feel if your love energy wants to - or wants not to - spread by imagining it in motion, flowing outward. Start by feeling it in the center of your heart, then guiding it outwards towards your surroundings, a certain situation, or a person. You can also chat with your love and ask, "Do you want to be spread?"

What is your love doing or saying? Is it spreading with ease and flow, without any resistance? If so, you know with certainty that it is right for you to share and spread. This IS pure connected-ness.

Is the energetic essence of your love not spreading easily, or with resistance—or only because you force it to spread? Then sharing is not in your best interest. Spreading it anyways is a disconnected-ness by you running yourself empty. A better way, is to let your love

BE and stay in your heart—creating a connected-ness.

The reasons behind why your love does not want to spread, can be many. You might be running low yourself and have nothing to give right now; it could simply be that sharing with this situation, surrounding, or person is not the best investment for you—not in alignment with your soul essence, or you might not be aligned with yourself in the purest way. The point is, it's not good for you and would push you into a disconnected-ness.

This wisdom is yours to feel, heal, and to shift into being your unquestioned knowing.

End this precious time with gratitude and love, and let yourself travel back into your now. Do this gently and with an unhurried agenda.

Breathe, and feel how you shifted as your woman into wholesomeness, knowing, enjoyment, and hopefully incredible excitement to trot down the street in your new day as your powerful female YOU! Time to get going, and move through your new NOW!

Take this practice to heart, realize how accurate it is, and never question the answers because your heart and your love is always right.

Be kind. Be smart. Be helpful. Be real. *Be a good person!*

FIND JOY IN EASY-PEASY-NESS

"Thank you, Captain Obvious!"

I can already see you going "Duh!" because who in the world would disagree with that title?

Yet, we are so imprinted with the wrongful truth of:

• It has to be hard in order to be good—just think how hard you are always working, yet making and baking a bread the harder way won't make it taste better. It is the same for your life.

• Good people are doing the "hard grind"—but doing the body function number two - pooping - when it is hard won't make you a good person and is definitely not a good feeling at all. No truth here.

• You have to work hard in order to receive good—best example I can think of is working out hard at the "sweat hole" - the gym - and injuring my body because I worked too hard. Ouch!

• Nothing that comes easy is of best value—well, breathing is normally really easy and life-saving, valuable as gold indeed.

• If it's easy, you are not doing a good enough job—I am writing this book pretty easily and I dare you to say that it's not a fantastic job. Easy means you are aligned with your inner wisdom, and you are giving it all you got.

• Life is hard—that is an old and stinky physical life feeling, and saying, that only has a worth when you are not in alignment with your energetic essence.

Must I go on? It's pretty clear that we are beating ourselves up silly over here because it's never about the "what" that you do, it's always about the "how."

Our old old recordings, habits, and beliefs are playing with our mind—creating bogus hints of "easy is bad," and we are playing it over and over like an old song that just won't get kicked out of the radio station.

I say let's kick it—by switching to a really well-feeling new belief of, "easy means aligned with my soul being, easy is key, easy is all there is, and easy is my new normal."

Say, think, and feel the following often:

- "It is so easy to BE me!"
- "It is so easy to live ME!"

Make singing your new belief, and dancing to it, a new well-feeling song that you can't get enough of. Make it your purpose to BE and live in easy-peasy-ness—read more about *purpose* in the chapter **What is Your Purpose in This Physical Life?**

"But what if it's hard? Is it still meant to BE?" you might ask…

Yes! Absolutely! If you really want it, it is meant to BE for you. You make your own reality. If your wish is hard to become real, it means that you have resistance towards allowing it to BE—a lot of the time because of your constant old song of, "it has to be hard." So instead of letting go of the hard-to-come wishes, let go of your resistance by singing and dancing to your new song of "It's so darn easy!" over and over, then expect your desires to join into your "easy" singing and dancing… Let's see what happens! I see the both of you, hand in hand and as one, living happily ever after. Hurray!

Easiness really suits you, because it lets you BE and live the "sweetness" of just being you—without the hard sweat-working-nonsense that turns your sweet into your sour.

Be kind. Be smart. Be helpful. Be real. *Be a good person!*

THE WORD "NO!"

The female world asks: "When did it ever start being OK for men, or anyone really, to not take a 'No!' from a woman - or any person or being - and run over it like it's nothing?" This is a real scenario that does happen, and one that I know you can relate to.

Still to this day, I encounter situations like that in numerous ways. I say "No!" to a deal in a store, the man does not take it. I say "No!" to a new membership package at the gym, the man does not hear it. I say "No!" and men - sometimes also women and children - don't hear it. Why?

One day the lightbulb went off and I realized that I am saying the word "no" timidly—because of my old beliefs, recordings, and ancient habits. Back in time, a little girl saying "no" was not necessarily the right thing to say, so when I dared to say it, it was very timid.

Let's take it even further. In the older generation's youthful time - sure as a door knob can turn - it was not fine for women to say "No!" and mean it. Since we are all eternal energy and share our energies with each other, we are naturally filled with ancestral feelings, thoughts, behaviors, habits, and old recordings - all energies - of their relationship with the word "no"—with the way they said it or thought about it. Timid, powerless, forbidden, or not at all.

Feel the difference of the poles apart energies of a "no," and each resulting outcome:

• Saying "No!" based off the energy of old recordings— calls for a weak outcome

• Saying "No!" based off the energetic value of being a powerful female essence, which has a clear "stop and enough" hammer attached—a good mid-sized meteorite outcome

• Saying "No!" based off the energetic value of really calibrating as a female energy, aligned with the absolute energetic value of the word "no, stop, enough, end of story, freeze"—a guaranteed sledgehammer that is felt all around the world

Saying "No!" with the energetic essence and meaning of the word itself while being absolutely aligned with ME has changed my life, and it shifted the world around me. It's a healing act of re-writing my old beliefs, while creating a betterment and well-being on my cellular level, that is one with consciousness.

Here is another way of looking at it: A "no" without energetic power or charged with the energetic value of "timid, forbidden, wrong," is like a sports car without a powerful motor, or going to a ball without a regal dress. It won't work, it is not fun, and the outcome is not as expected.

On the contrary, a "no" with the sureness of "I mean it!" will be an immediate stop for anyone in the vicinity, hearing it—heck, even all the way across the planet they will feel it.

You might say… "Sure, but others should take my no either way."

You are right! Others should take your "No!" without you going into a huge effort to present it the right way. No debate there.

So then why are you the one who has to change in order to be respected? Because it's you who is bothered by your "No!" not being respected, and it's you who is unhappy with how it is going so far. It is you who is in charge of you!

Counting on others to change, or waiting for change to happen, shifts you into a lower victim-type of frequency—which is nothing else than an old habit of you asking to be treated better. You are giving your power away, a very fragile way to create betterment that keeps you stagnant and not expanding, the exact opposite of what you came here to do and BE. Plus, by wanting others to change so you can feel better while staying as you are, is a growth and rising-in-maturity opportunity missed.

Then there is the waiting until you have grey hair fact… Surely you don't want to waste your time in such a silly way.

I suggest for you to make use of the tremendous power that you possess: energetically align with your soul essence - the biggest, most powerful, and wisest part of you - by taking responsibility for how you feel, how you carry yourself, and how you choose to show up as a result of that. Then, as that power you say "No!" It's the only real way to use the word "no" meaningfully; it's the only way to demonstrate and teach the use of "no" to your children; it's the only real way to orchestrate the world around you into a space where you are heard, felt, seen, and thought of.

Here is a feeling roller-coaster and real eye-opener "no" experience I had the privilege to be a part of. I turned it into a fairytale story since it's just us girls…

Once upon a time…

I encountered a beautiful older woman sitting on a bench. I was inspired to gift her my book **365 Days of Happiness**, with the thought that she would really enjoy my book circling through my head and heart.

No worries, no need to call the doctor. I get inspired to do things like this all the time, knowing that there is something in this experience for me—yet this time it was not what I had thought it would be.

I fetched a paperback from my car. As I walked back to the bench I was so excited that I literally calibrated myself into the highest form of high-for-life feelings for this co-creation and explosion of goodness to happen—to spread all around the world and beyond.

Once I stood next to the lady, I said, "Hi, I think you would really like my book." She would not even look at me. Then, with ferocious eyes and a tone that could fell even the most rock solidly rooted tree, she said "No!"

In confusion, I replied, "I wrote this book, that's why I would like to give it to you." Again, she was not having any of me or my book and said "Whatever! No! I don't want it! I don't care!"

I was able to mutter a very tiny, "OK! Have a great day…" while walking away in puzzlement.

Then I asked my physical self, my soul being, and the whole universe, "How in the world can my energetic guidance and inspiration to give her the book be so off?"

At first I felt hurt, and then a bit angry that she would treat me like that. However, I shifted to knowing that those are my feelings, and that she did not give them to me or make me feel that way.

I started to talk the situation through with my physical self, my soul being, and the universe. It went something like this:

"What the bleep just happened and why???"

"Well Jacqueline, this would have made you feel amazing, maybe even loved and appreciated, and also given you the worth of being a good person, but she didn't want to be your tool or 'staircase to heaven' to feel good. That's not her job. It's your job! Take responsibility and let her go by taking care of yourself—by shifting to feeling good without this encounter being a feel-good one."

My next feeling, was starting to feel sorry for her and thinking how hard it must be when your heart is so hardened that you can't receive a gift—I even went as far as feeling sorry for the whole world, because there was clearly something wrong with the world. I took the liberty to send her love, and practiced loving her and the whole world.

That is when my physical me, my soul me, and my consciousness hit me like a missile—I had it all wrong, and woman, was I in a selfish place right then.

That beautiful older woman was a strong and powerful woman! She was a very determined being who stood up for what was right for her at that moment. She did it without budging an inch to make me happy. She knew what she wanted - or in my case what she did not want - and made it incredibly clear that she would not have any of it. She had her own mind and said her "No!" exactly as it is supposed to be used— strong, forceful, and with an undeniable "I mean it!"

That brought me to ask myself, "Who am I to expect anything from her or ask for her to make me feel good when it's not her responsibility to act a certain way, or to take my offering? And who am I to feel sorry for her - or the whole world - and send pity-love because I assume that her heart is hardened, or that something is wrong, just because she said her 'No!'?"

"Giving someone a gift and sending someone love is OK, but expectations and pity-love? Really Jacqueline? You know better than that!" the universe informed me.

Was she unkind? No! She was very kind to herself. That IS where pure kindness starts.

It was not her. It was me who had it all wrong. It was me needing to feel good and it was me who judged her heart. And yes, it was me who sent pity-love. She was just sitting on a bench being herself, and knowing what she wanted and defending her space with the utmost powerful soul guidance that she knew was right for her.

Would she have enjoyed my book of happiness? Yes, I am sure of that. But that is not the point here.

I learned a mountainous amount about me, my life, and the expansion I am here to calibrate into. I untangled my old beliefs of gifting and the need to make me feel good, of judging others who are actually really happy as they are, and to only take every single experience for what it is for ME. I learned to not dig in other's gardens of what it is for them, because either I will mess their gardens up with the outcome of no growth, or they mess mine up pretty good, as that lady did. Then again, she dug so deep that a replanting of my garden happened right there on the spot. "So thanks, lady!"

I also learned what a real meaningful "No!" can be or IS—I definitely copy that. What a golden opportunity for me to expand, grow, and heal as ME!

She was strong willed. She knew what she wanted. She was not to be messed with. She IS a powerful woman! That is definitely what "BEing a woman" IS all about.

Be kind. Be smart. Be helpful. Be real. *Be a good person!*

WOMEN—THEY GO IN GROUPS

Maybe I just never got the women-group-thing, or the group thing never got me—because after all it is always an exchanging co-creation. Be it finding a women-group in which I can receive support by talking over problems, situations, and fed-up-ness or one in which I can practice something happy, like a hobby, talk energy, or hang out as moms... I just never found satisfaction in any of it. On the other hand, having fun with my very good women-friends - as a duo or little group - I always enjoy.

For the longest time I thought, well, I am just not made of the same clay than these groups or maybe I am a "verklemmt" lady, one who can't hang out with a female crowd.

Only later in life did I realize why I am not a mass-fitting-in-er. Maybe this is you too! So I thought I would bring it up in this book, because the norm, the normal, and the well-understood way is that women do go in groups.

First off, no matter what you choose or what you like - groups or not - you can in fact always feel fine about your preferences because the rule here is that if it is OK for you, it is of a complete OK-nature—no matter what others might say or do. You always know what is best for you. End of story. This leaves the only question that needs to be asked, which is, "Am I OK with it?"

I can honestly say that my biggest priority is always - and was since I was a small child - that I am an only-with-my-soul aligned being—without space for anybody else to mix in on my soul level. Of course, on my physical life level there is lots of mix-and-matching going on—that is after all what I am here for as my woman. If you must, ask my family. They know that I am pretty radical about this pureness—even when choosing the perfect coffee, food, and wine. They can vouch and are witnesses that when I am not pure, I am miserable, or when the wine is not perfect I won't drink it. But no worries, I'll cook with it instead.

I made a point in both of my books, **365 Days of Happiness** and **Parenting Through the Eyes of Lollipops**, to highlight the fact that everyone should be a radically only-with-my-soul aligned being—as that is what everyone's right to existence IS, and what everyone came here to experience. Kids too!

When younger, I thought that my only-with-my-soul aligned being was of a negative nature. I tried to change it and was made to change, every time with the result of physical unwell-ness. Then I started to understand and accept my radical-being-me as my wonderful self-love mechanism, a super smart action of the harmonious dance between my soul being and my physicality if you ask me.

My only-with-my-soul aligned being was always strong, being super sensitive from the beginning—and got even more fine-tuned through my abuses. I have to say, I got amazing practice to persistently BE and live it. Being so sensitive, I had to constantly make space for me or else I felt it physically, and the abuses highlighted a clear overcrowded-ness in my soul-space, hinting that I better get pure again—which I did after each episode. These repeating scenarios made me a master in being a not mass-fitting-in-er.

When things get too impure or too crowded for me I swerve too far away from my pure me. That is when I leave—physically if possible, but soulfully always. Once out, I shift back to purifying my pure-me through consciously feeling my soul essence.

Many times I hear myself saying loud and clear before even entering a situation, "This is not the group or event that you want to go to!" Mostly I answer by not going, and that's when I am smart… However, sometimes I overstep my soul and go anyways—a choice with consequences. The good news is that I am getting smarter and smarter each time.

I know that it is OK that I am not a mass-person and it is just fine that I am not fitting in with the group orientation, the norm, the normal, and what's expected of me, because I fit in with my soul being. That is all that matters!

If this sounds like you, I invite you to make jolly peace with who you are, and find excitement in the knowing that you ARE in fact OK as IS. You ARE awesome as IS!

If this is not you and you ARE a fan of women groups and gatherings, then I applaud you to keep such a valuable female-group-energy vibrating—creating a place where women can find themselves, hear themselves, have fun, and BE themselves. You are awesome too!

Bottom line is that if it's OK for you, it is always OK!

Be kind. Be smart. Be helpful. Be real. *Be a good person!*

AUTHENTICITY

Everyone talks about being authentic nowadays, and in the right way, that is indeed very powerful; powerful for the world by you bringing across what you are made of, and powerful for you by speaking about who you are—while constantly finding a new you that you can talk about.

I truly enjoy anyone who shows their truth and bona fide selves with clarity, strength, and is speaking their ways loud and clear—even if they yell it out. It is also important for me to shout out that I respect everyone who is authentic no matter the how, what, who, or where.

However, how real and *what type of real* do you really want it to be?

Some types of authenticity are not the greatest power for the one speaking it—when not feeling high-for-life happy while, about, and after being authentic, it means it's not of pure intention and not of ultimate power. Often this dis-alignment will initiate an unwell questioning of the reaction received to what authenticity has been spoken of.

There is a simple explanation for this energetically, while also making sense in physical life.

Authentically speaking or expressing oneself through the truth of one's own positivity is the only way the truth-mission is a well-feeling one, the result being, you feel amazing and your surroundings react with respect since your positive authenticity - your pure positive energy - IS what you are made of, always available for you to plug into, and here to focus your full momentum on.

Why? You make the world a better space by sharing your zeal with everyone and everything. Not saying that all will love it or drop to your feet and adore you, but they will either respect the force your positivity has by leaving you as is, or they will be forced by your positivity to move aside—at the very least it won't scratch you a bit if someone opposes you, because your positivity outshines their negativity. This is authenticity at it's best!

More often than not, however, we cut our power and validation short by not speaking our positive truth, by letting it be unspoken; instead, choosing to express ourselves by speaking about the negative untruth of what we experience, we despise, and want gone. Or even worse, we try to be authentic by being against something or someone. Not only is this giving that of what is unwanted grand energetic momentum and a tempo that is hard to control, it will also be hard to shift back to positivity from such a point.

Negativity is a choice only existing in physicality. Energetically, there is no negative, and since the physical world is literally polarized towards it, negativity has this natural way of spreading super fast and into giganticness. Negativity is a very old and untrue habit and is oftentimes practiced because it's more comfortable for people. Let's face it, how easy is it to get lost in the initial reaction of "double doo-doo on you-you," and right after realizing that the negative-you just won the race. That right there is a great representation of old recordings!

Sticking with negativity does not ask the world to see how much more positive it could be and does not ask for a change into a more truthful positive authenticity. Result being, we stay way too cozy and don't grab for better.

We can change that by:

• Understanding that authenticity IS realizing we are all the same pure positive energy

• Knowing that we chose to come here into this physical life as women and have meaning to BE and live our purpose through our choices—here to create a positive life for ourselves and others

• BEing and living the fact that our whole sacred-ness - our energetic essence, our soul being, our higher-self, and our physicality - put together into one pot and mixed up real good, IS our authenticity

Claiming your positivity IS claiming your authenticity—claiming your authenticity IS claiming your positivity. This is a chicken and egg scenario, hard to choose which one comes first. The outcome is the same; authenticity!

How do you measure if you really are your authentic you right now? Well, how does the way you ARE and express yourself feel?

If how you feel has the slight flavor of frustration or a spice of "I'll show them," then it is clearly not your authentic self—it will only feel good for a split second followed closely by unwell feelings. If you are angry... I think we don't need to cover which bucket that fits into.

If you feel good, you are aligned with your authentic you. Keep in mind to check in with yourself daily, sometimes even hourly, because you are an ever-changing energetic positivity-clump that is vibrating in an energetic ever-changing universe. Staying stagnant results in not feeling good anymore, meaning you lost your alignment with your authenticity.

The bottom line is that if you feel 100% good in who you are right now, you are indeed authentically aligned—this is the best barometer since your purpose, as we cover in the chapter **What is Your Purpose in This Physical Life?** is to feel good.

Another great way to look at it is...

Your soul being would never waste time or energy - even though running out of energy is never the problem - to talk, think, say, act, hear, smell, taste, and feel negativity, as it does not exist in an essence of pure positive energy. Negativity is an only-in-physical-life choice that you can either indulge in and give your life legacy to, or handle as your real super positive power, "What negativity? Never heard of it! Then again, I don't pay much attention to wasteful stuff."

This asks you to refrain from wanting to snatch a taste of old habits or other people's habits, instead, it's asking you to keep surfing in your high-for-life wave of pure positivity—your authenticity.

Important! True authenticity is never based on "negativing" anything or anyone. It never has anything or anyone besides you included in it. It is never against anything or anyone but always only as you, and for you. As that being of authenticity, you are in fact real aligned power, through which everything IS always possible.

You are the only one who has a ticket to be at the show of your authenticity. It IS, in fact, a private event!

Be kind. Be smart. Be helpful. Be real. *Be a good person!*

LGBTQ—AND SOME SEX-SENSE FOR ALL

Strange that we even have to talk about people being themselves, when all we are meant to do here in this physical life is BE and live ourselves—happily, that is. But, since it needs to be brought up and in order to celebrate all beings, I decided I might as well write a whole chapter about it and for it.

I can't start in any other way than saying, "Bravo for living your truth, LGBTQs!"

Now that's out of the way, what was the point again? See, it is still weird to have to make a case here, to dissect these different sexual behaviors and really talk about what is normal… Whatever "normal" people say, that is, and whatever they are basing it on.

I say let's base my book on love, because that is what everyone is looking for, what everyone wants, what always works no matter what, what makes sense for everyone, and what never fails.

So here we go love—I know you have my back!

I'll start with the fact that you chose to BE a woman, by either coming into this physical life as a woman - even if changing to be a man later in life - or changing to the female gender at some point. Fact is that at a certain time you chose to BE a woman.

Not leaving men out here, but after all this book is for women—however, the points I am about to make are true for men loving men, men deciding to be women, and women shifting to be men too. Keep reading…

Arriving as a female means your soul essence made sure that you are experiencing the start of your life as a girl.

Embrace that fact! For learning more about your female reasons read the chapter **Why a Woman and Not a Man?**

Deciding to change into a woman after a while means your soul essence is making sure that you are experiencing your further life as a woman. Embrace that shift by digging into the beginning of my book where it talks about the female physical existence in detail.

I cannot stress enough the truth of this: There is never anything wrong and nothing ever went wrong if you are a woman who loves women, if you are a woman changing to be a man, or if you are a man transforming into a woman. Your preferences are never an accident or miscalculation on your part, your soul part, your physical part, or on life's part. You always choose your female existence with the purest purpose of aligning with who you are and to feel good. How much better can it get?

Being sexually oriented in your unique and creative ways and living your blissful sexuality fully and vividly, or born a gender then changing, is the same as having red hair, different skin colors, having different origins, talking in various languages, or being a baker or a mail man.

What difference do these dissimilarities make, in the big picture of everyone and everything being here to experience physical life as the same energetic beings with the same purpose—to BE and live, in a way that feels right and happy, and to expand as such to calibrate all consciousness?

There is no difference!

No breaking news here. Yet, for many there is trouble on the horizon, even anger and judgement. Some might close this book right here—maybe even rip or burn it. Not to give you ideas…

I fully understand that this way of living, seeing, thinking, feeling, and being is not everyone's cup of sexuality, but isn't love everyone's teapot? From that base of love, a space where we can all meet and learn from each other, I ask you to please bear with me while I make a real good talking point here.

My teachings are never based on religion, faith, or judging the differences, they are based on everyone and everything being the same pure positive energy - love - and having the same reasons to be here, to experience physical life in order to learn about humanity and expand into "more and happy" while at it—to make the energy wheel go round and round.

LGBTQ soul beings chose to come here to experience what they said they will get a taste of when pushing the "Go" button—and here they are, creating and having exactly that. And just like everyone else, they are good little soldiers to their inner guidance, following what is right for them—to love in their fitting way.

That is wonderful, and can only be applauded loudly, because by doing so they live their meaning and expand in their purpose by being true to who they are. To some degree, this is more than I can say for many non-LGBTQ people.

They are helping all of consciousness because they provoke diversity, new-ness, different than old and antique, and a freshness—they bring forth an expansion of the universe that would not BE if they not ARE. They help everyone evolve, even if you don't like them or their way of living. You are learning and are pushed to explore something outside of your comfort zone. Heck, you are presented with an opportunity to form an opinion about life in itself. That creates new thoughts in and for you—you become a better and "more" of you. In my eyes, a huge "Thank you!" is in order, no matter if you agree with their ways of living or not.

In any case, what right does anyone have to either agree or disagree with someone's truth? And where does this right-taking come from when you have nothing to do with other people's truth, but only are responsible for living your own?

This is a clear overstepping, and a wrongly pointed focus!

It's like you decide to watch you favorite movie - your life - and while it's playing while you are alive, instead of watching, you are staring at the white wall to your left. You will miss your life, your focus, your purpose—and you will miss out on your movie. Then the movie is over, and you say, "Well that was empty!" Of course it's empty if you are focusing on other's lives when there is nothing there that is of your concern, and it's not your place to look. Whereas your life... Wow! When you look at it with your complete focus, it's the most fulfilling movie ever.

I say, "Forget the white wall by letting it be as white as it IS, and wants to BE!"

Besides, looking at anyone else's truth by dissecting what they are doing, or what they are not doing, takes your focus off your purpose of realizing your own happiness. The promise you made to yourself and to all of consciousness when *why* you chose to come into this physical life, stays unfulfilled. Instead, you are creating dis-alignment and unhappiness that you share with the whole world and beyond. This might read harsh but it is the truth—your truth if you choose that path.

A better investment for yourself and your time here is to celebrate ALL of love instead. That means celebrate ALL beings.

Asking anyone - LGBQ and straight - to suppress their true pleasure of sexuality, is undermining these true desires that originate from the truest essence that we all ARE—which is pure positive energy, soul beings. Not living, expressing, enjoying, and blissfully experiencing sexuality the way that fits and is of well-feeling nature for a person, means that they are not living a purpose of creating happiness—and are not helping all of us one-consciousness beings, instead spreading and sharing unhappiness with everyone and everything.

In the case of the LGBTQs, it's like getting an energetic slap when an LGBTQ being is not able to BE and live as they wish. And there goes another energetic slap, and another and another... Whereas, instead of a downing slap, it could be an uplifting energetic hug.

It's not hard to figure out what has to be done!

If we go really basic here, normally we say to people, "Make yourself happy and live a nice life!" There is no difference for LGBTQs.

"Make yourself happy and live a nice life!"

LGBTQs are important for the human cycle of life the same way that every other living being is—the ones you like and the ones you don't like, all are important. We need them! We need you! We need everyone—to make the energetic wheel of consciousness go round and round.

Fact is, living your sexuality, celebrating the beauty of it, and feeling the pure emotions of this natural energizing capability that physicality gifts us with, means that you are in fact exercising the purpose you promised to BE and live when you chose to show up as your woman you, your LGBTQ you, your man you—your whole you.

The pureness in energy that is created by the sacred act of making and feeling love - alone or in partnership - IS a direct alignment with the glory of who you really are. It IS a high-for-life frequency.

Of course the how, what, when, where, and with whom, always has to be chosen as OK by every single person involved—any overstepping is abuse and not OK. No exceptions ever!

If it makes you happy and you are not hurting anyone or anything, or bringing danger to the world, you are expanding and are of the utmost beneficial service to all of consciousness. Your "happy you" matters, by making the world a better place!

You literally mean the world, to the world!

So you tell me what the energetic and humanitarian value of LGBTQ people are—I say, it is humongous!

This chapter is to celebrate all of love—to celebrate all of YOU, LGBTQ and straight ones alike!

Be kind. Be smart. Be helpful. Be real. *Be a good person!*

DECISIONS

Decision making is always a subject carrying enormous weight in the female world of BEing and living. Might even feel the heebie-jeebies become alive when deciding…

Why is that so?

It stems from all past experiences you had and also the ones the whole world, in a time before you, had. Just think how non-existent decision-making was for women back in time.

It was either a non-happening or a happening with great consequences—add to that your little girl factor of how many times you were asked for your opinion to help decide a family option, or how many times you were able to decide for yourself when you were little. How many times did other people decide for you?

No matter how much time has passed and how many decisions you are making today, without getting conscious awareness of this and actually shifting your old recordings, you still are carrying that troubled energetic-decision-essence in you, for you, and with you.

I say, it's about high-time to let that go!

How? Become consciously aware of every decision that you make—the tiniest all the way to the humongous ones. All of them! Then ask, "Through what energy am I making this decision?"

For example:

When you choose to set your alarm for the next day - that is a decision - ask yourself, "Through what energy am I making the decision to set the alarm for this certain time?"

Of course it is clear that you are choosing this alarm to be on time for your new day, but what energy, what feelings, are you BEing and living while you are choosing?

Are you feeling angry that you have to get up that early? That indicates a sense of being overpowered, told what to do, and wishing for freedom to choose yourself.

Are you scared that if you are late you will lose your job or get bad grades in class? That brings up a sense of being overruled and told "you better, or else," or that you can't be yourself because it has scary consequences.

Are you rethinking your choice of time over and over? That brings up the energetic essence of "you better not make a mistake," and, "can I really decide, am I capable to decide?"

This exercise will inform you of all the old recordings, beliefs, and habits that you are making your decisions from. Becoming aware of them and shifting them out of your life means that your decisions will flow with your purest of truths—I am here to BE and live fittingly for myself by making my own fitting decisions!

Other great questions to ask yourself when making a decision are: "Is this decision shifting me to be *little* or does it let me stay *big*, and is the outcome of my decision making me feel *little* or *big*?"

If *little* is your answer, you are making the decision from your plateau of being your little girl because you are energetically BEing and living your *little* you right now—deciding from there. That decision momentum, and the outcome, will not be aligned with your truth of who you are now—your big you.

If your answer is *big*, then you are on the right track to make good and fitting decisions that bring you further in your whole being—as your *big* you that you are now. Bravo!

Bottom line is, deciding for your woman as your little child won't work, just as standing up for your woman from the space of being your little child won't work either.

You can see how loaded with "back in time" and upbringing energies a decision can be, and how you can fine-tune your choices to make the decision-making process a healing one—one that represents who you really are right now.

I see this as phenomenal because it lets you shift decision-making to be something normal, easy, and small—no matter the impact of the decision. It will become like drinking a glass of water… Important but no need to spend hours and hours on deciding the "what, how, when and where." You are thirsty—fill a glass of water, bless the water, and drink it with gratitude. End of that decision!

In other words, acknowledge the situation, look at your options, feel into them, decide with gratitude and conviction. End of decision, moving on to the next.

After the decision is made, you can then treat the new-ness that you just created with special magic by blessing the outcome with love, kindness, and laughter—even celebrating it with an inside soul-party or something bigger, like a party with friends.

Know that, in case your decision was not the best after all, you can always decide new right then and there. At the time of your decision you did the best you could with the understanding you had.

By not looking back at what you could have done better, and instead looking forward to decide new by feeling into your new options and picking with gratitude, you make decision-making easy. This way you decide through your *big* you! Again, party like there is no tomorrow, knowing that you just created a phenomenal new-ness for yourself. No harm done and on you go.

Most decisions can be changed and replaced by a new decision at any time—there is never anything big or serious going on. Rather, it is all easy-peasy life stuff—just like drinking water.

Give yourself permission to decide freely and lightheartedly—no matter the importance of anything or anyone. Deciding IS a lot of fun—so make it a lot of fun!

Be kind. Be smart. Be helpful. Be real. *Be a good person!*

COMPASSION AND EMPATHY

Do you feel bad when something goes wrong for others, or even live their suffering fully and vividly? Do you maybe even bathe in it and feel like a good girl by saying with pride, "I am a compassionate empath?" And is it so, even when your life is phenomenal and you had nothing do do with their happenings—at most, you even tried to help but it went wrong anyways?

I could go on and on with examples because that was me - and sometimes still is - until I realized how wrong and unwell it all feels. So I asked myself, "What is the right way to be compassionate and empathetic, so I feel well? Versus feeling unwell and mostly relating to things of negative nature."

Fact is that the compassion and empathy of "feeling bad" for someone, or something, is not aiding you in your whole well-being and definitely not helping the one who is deeply and up to their knees in a pain that they are trying to figure out or clean up. Remember, you are one with everything and everyone, sharing and spreading your essence of "feeling bad" to all, making yourself sick and their load even heavier. These are real consequences staring you in the face here! The result being that all is unwell and nothing is solved.

"Feeling bad" is the opposite of your nature and a distortion of who you - and all - truthfully are—pure positive energy. Your personal unwell feelings are a clear sign of you going the wrong way in your one-way journey to happiness. However, since these bad feelings are yours, it is still a truthful expansion of yourself because you learn how to turn around and go from unwell to well again.

Feeling bad for something or someone and living their pain is a different story, though. These are not your feelings to feel and heal—they will be hard to digest. Think of eating another person's fatty meal when for you a lean meal is your perfect food. The digestion process will be harder.

Feeling someone else's pain fills every cell of your whole being with an energy that is not fitting for you, because it's not yours. From there it is really hard, and endlessly exhausting, to help yourself or others, let alone to shift back to feeling better and aligned with yourself. Whereas if you only feel what is yours, you are able to claim it, deal with it, cleanse it, and heal it. The digestion is easy and the expansion truthful—the outcome of a bigger, better, and "more" you is natural.

Here is another way of looking at it:

"Since you have a headache, let me hit myself with a frying pan so I have a headache too!" Not sure how much sense this makes, since now there are two doofuses with a painful head who can't help each other because both are laying on the sofa, not able to get up to make tea.

Some good questions to ask yourself, and to get you on your truthful path, are:

• Why am I entertaining other people's low energies by feeling and living them deeply?

• Why am I not just acknowledging what they are going through and stop right after that?

• Why am I not aligning with my roots of pure positive energy?

Many times the reason why we practice negative compassion and empathy is because of old recordings, racked up from childhood—from others saying things like:

• To feel for people is being kind.

• To feel better than the ones suffering is wrong.

• Keep your happiness restrained… Because what might others think?

• Make sure that you are not too much or over the top.

Add the flavor of always having been supposed to be a good girl by showing respect - through feeling for others - and we have a perfectly old, moldy, and untruthful pie that simply is yuck—and probably never tasted good from the beginning.

However there is a real good, truthful way to feel and use compassion and empathy. Makes sense, since there is always a phenomenal way to experience anything and everyone in your physical life in order to expand and calibrate further into your truth. Why else would something be?

Go into a selfish and ignoring denial, a space where you can take care of yourself in a self-centered, unapologetic way to be the happiest YOU that you can be. There, practice fully positive compassion and empathy for yourself—while denying all negative and feel-bad feelings that others carry, and are always available.

That way you can show up as the saving hero, while everyone else lives life "beaten to the maximum" and are laying on the curb of your journey to more and more happiness. Without ever leaving your journey, you can then hand out positive compassion and empathy of appreciation, respect, gratitude, and love—but have the sufferers come to your happy path to fetch it, not the other way around. That is the only way you can lend anyone or anything a hand while still staying well.

On the other hand, if someone is a shiner - a super connected, aligned, happy person - who is flying in a high-for-life frequency, latch on and feel positive compassion and empathy for them fully and vividly. Jump on, go for a piggy-back-ride, fly high together, and never let go!

Compassion and empathy for others coming from a relationship with oneself - versus from a non-relationship with oneself - is the only way these feelings are of well-feeling nature. It is how to be a truthful compassionist and empath!

Feeling the best in you and for others, living the best in you and for others, seeing the best in you and for others, and wishing the best in you and for others, is the only potent way for yourself and for others to expand and create a phenomenal life—remember, we are all connected as one and share energy at all times. You are a powerful creator—for your own life, for the lives of other people, and for all of consciousness.

Betterment, world change, a shift in situations, and helping people—it all starts with you claiming your well-feeling positivity, then BEing, living, and showing your positive compassion and empathy to and for yourself, as well as to and for others.

This IS the real way to feel compassion and empathy.

Be kind. Be smart. Be helpful. Be real. *Be a good person!*

NOTHING AND NOBODY NEEDS TO CHANGE FOR YOU

And why would it anyway since you are always expanding with whatever IS? Not to mention, if you desire change, you can make it happen. You are the creator with the potential to put unlimited momentum on whatever it is that you want, without ever needing to wait for said change to arrive. Pretty cool if you ask me!

I am indeed a very impatient woman. Just ask, those who know me will slap their hand to their foreheads with a clear, "Yep, Jacqueline is so impatient, she can't wait for anything, instead she'll just go make it happen."

That is because I am very connected with my soul essence, trusting the guidance I receive, and know when to give gas to my momentum. From the outside, it looks like I am a wild woman on a mission, but from the inside it IS alignment. When my solid focus works I know that I am in sync with who I am—in full power because of that. When it doesn't, I take full responsibility for the fail even if others are involved. It is still my dis-alignment that made the fail happen.

Something about that fail though... Many times what looks like a fail at the start, shows itself as a gift in disguise, because something much more fitting and better needed to happen— something that I could not grasp while in my unconnected way. Me, re-aligning with who I am, always lets the "better" arrive freely. Like the time when I cooked a cheese sauce, and instead of it melting into a dreamy creamy-ness, the cheese showed me its clear disagreement by separating into liquid and a mass of cheese. Yuck! Then I ran like a mad scientist trying to find edible things to make it bind together again, because hey, we had hungry guests. At the end I succeeded and learned quite a bit about how the cheese liked to roll. The result of this being, I found a new favorite way to make cheese sauce—a happy end indeed.

So why does nothing and nobody need to change for you?

For one, you can make whatever you want to happen, happen, even if the situation or the person stays in their stubborn unchanged ways. There is no need to waste your energy on changing the *who* or *it* through hard work or convincing.

Secondly, when you are truly aligned with your soul being, understand your meaning, and focus on your purpose to create happiness, the world around you can go up in flames—without it mattering to you. Actually, the flames can give you the perfect stage to practice staying in your alignment, making you more powerful. Acknowledging the flames without judgement and letting all your feelings initiated by these flames come up freely, gives you understanding of who you are. Respecting, accepting, appreciating, thanking, and loving them, helps you cleanse and letting this new found wisdom be of immense value. All while connected and happy, expanding in your true ways and calibrating perfectly for you—the way you promised yourself to BE when choosing to come into your physical life, to make all of the collective consciousness richer as a whole.

Needing anything to change for you would rob you of these benefits and water down your experience of physical life to a point where asking, "Why have a half full bathtub when you could have the whole ocean with all its bounty?" is of value. I personally will always choose the ocean and the wildness of the bountiful adventure—sometimes that adventure is napping on the couch and sometimes it is going to the ocean, but never does the couch or the ocean have to change to be richer and better for me. If needed I'll make it change to work for me, as I explain plentifully in my book **365 Days of Happiness**—for 365 days that is.

I invite you to give up the need to demand change in others or situations. Instead, connect with yourself, and from there go and create the change you wish to be by demonstrating loudly FOR what you want - never against what you don't want - or by singing and dancing alone or with your children and loved ones, and not giving a care in the world.

This allows you to feel good and be happy even when others behave badly, because you know the trick of practicing an absolute connection to your well-being—not to mention, your stubborn unwillingness to feel bad. Other people's tantrums will shift to either be of profound humor for you, or the way they behave won't matter—and if you wish, from that space, you can help them.

The truth is, it is all about your relationship with your soul being, your relationship with yourself, and never about the relationship you have with others!

Life IS a playground—play in it!

Be kind. Be smart. Be helpful. Be real. *Be a good person!*

EXPECTATIONS

Your expectations are the power-wand that you were looking for because expectation is an energy with loads of momentum, like a high-speed rocket that is shot into the sky saying, "Right now, this is what I want!"

So watch your expectations, since expecting something a certain way attracts exactly that because on a cellular level, you are programming yourself to vibrate in the frequency of your expectation—and the universe loves to assure a perfect match made in heaven.

Most of the time we expect the worst or at least the negative result—followed by surprise when it goes exactly as we had expected it. This screams of old recordings, old beliefs, and old habits all the way. I invite you to consciously dig a little deeper here, and find all your unwell feeling expectations. Write them in a journal with the opposite, the positive, expectation right next to it. Use *those* in your further and forward life. Lots of practice will make you a perfectly positive-expectation-er! So, no slacking here!

If you expect men to disrespect you, it is an open invitation for things to happen in that way. If you expect something to go wrong, then it is almost a guarantee that it will. Naturally, if you expect positive outcomes, so BE it!

When you are expecting, it is best to consciously focus on only expecting the good, the most positive, and the best ever. The result being, you have a fat chance that that is what will happen. You set yourself up in good company that way, and you set others free of behaving badly. As a result you won't be drenched with the horse-dookie they have been giving you so far or any new *bad* that is expected to arrive.

You have a lot of control over what comes your way—expecting accordingly the "what" and "how" you want has potent value. It's like when you order the best food at your favorite restaurant, the chef will deliver the expectation—and so does the universe.

Questions like, "How would I like it to BE?" followed by saying, "I expect exactly this or that for me," is that pure power that I am writing about. Add in the feelings of how great you feel when what you expect will BE, visualize the perfectness of it all, and you have an irresistible momentum for yourself.

When - or better said if - something happens for you that is not as good as you want it to be, ask yourself, "What was my expectation?" Most often you will find that not only did you expect exactly that "not good thing," but you also felt it and maybe even visualized it.

Opening yourself up to the power of your positive expectations is a very potent and valuable practice. It puts you in charge and nourishes your trust in you, your energetic essence, and consciousness—in all of life, if you will.

Happy expecting!

Be kind. Be smart. Be helpful. Be real. *Be a good person!*

PROBLEM SHIFTING

Problem solving and shifting should always occur from the highest graciousness, the clearest, most powerful, deeply relaxed, and infinitely peaceful standpoint ever. Makes sense, since that space is called your 'concrete alignment' with who you are—and where your best wisdom for solutions lies.

Then, why is it that we try to find solutions and changes without first shifting into our highest soul space? Why is it, that while feeling low and sometimes at rock bottom, we go out and try to solve the world?

Many times we are present only in our physicality, and not in a balanced combination of energetically and physically. We either forget that we are first and foremost energetically wired, have never heard such a thing of "we are energy," or are simply not aware and focused enough to have that incredible connection, let alone able to keep it nourished and going.

It takes daily and sometimes focused, split-second work, and determined practice—yes! But the payoff of well-feeling, complete knowing, and clear understanding is invaluable, not to mention the energy conservation that is taking place for you because you don't have to find answers the hard way—just to find out that these "answers" were actually wrong for you.

Have a problem? Connect inward to your limitless soul power, listen to your incredible soul wisdom, then walk the walk of your "oh-so sweet and wonderful" soul journey while enjoying your soul passion. Funny, once there I often ask myself "What problem?" Not sure if it disappears, gets solved or shifts, or was imagined by my colorful mind. Fact is that, often, problems are not there once in alignment.

This connection is where you will be so powerful that, surely enough, some might ask for you to step down and be of "lesser power" by giving you even more problems, or rebelling against your clarity. That is when you know you made it!

Never mind them and certainly never become less. Instead, connect even deeper and stronger to keep walking your walk. Enjoy the nay-sayers with giggles and maybe even a finger or two by being focused, determined, and ruthlessly you. Also, never leave your soul path. Instead, widen your path, and if needed make a little shift to the right or left to keep it interesting. That's fine as long as you keep walking on your path of your soul journey, and ARE the truest power that you came here to BE, expand as, and calibrate into.

Solving real-life problems is a fact of life. One that, in the best way possible and with the most meaningful outcome for yourself and all women in the world, is always accomplished by BEing, living, showing up as, voicing and in some cases yelling, scratching, or by fighting from an energy of absolutely knowing of who you are—your connected and rock-solid being.

Versus fighting the fight for *who* you are, for *where* you stand, and for *what* you are—in that type of rebellion you are asking to be accepted, without it ever coming to the point of putting the spotlight onto what really matters, which is your desire to BE and live your truth. This is not a powerful way to create a better physical life experience for yourself and women as a whole. Instead:

• You want to fight for betterment, freedom, and respect as a fact of living this physical life and not from a focus of being a woman—because that's beside the point.

• You want to be rooted as a YOU—a whole being,

behaving like it's normal to BE your woman.

• You want to align with an energy where you don't need approval for who you are, don't need to ask for understanding for where you are, let alone desire acknowledgment for what you are—from anyone.

• You want to lay down the law through understanding yourself, because you know that this is the only understanding you will ever need in order to create change, shifts, and solve problems.

The result being, you feel powerful as you—as your energetic essence. That IS you!

FEELING BELITTLED

Feeling belittled is a funny thing, because if I would not know any better, I would say that this is your cue to acknowledge that you shifted into your energetic essence of being your little girl—versus being the grown woman that you are right now. Then again, I do know better and that is exactly what it is!

So, what's to dislike about this wonderful nudge to re-align and go spend some quality time with your inner girl—to embrace her with your loving thoughts and feelings until she pops like an over-filled love balloon? I say nothing!

When belittlement comes in and up for me, I acknowledge, accept, respect, appreciate, love, and thank this dear little friend with the most gracious smile by taking exceptional care of myself, my inner child, and my childhood journey. Some days, this means pampering myself with loving care in the form of a good cry, watching children play, or enjoying a beautiful movie. Other days, it is meditation, visualization, exercise, or a huge glass of red wine paired with dark chocolate. Ice cream works too!

I take advantage of knowing that I am responsible for my inner girl, and that nobody but me can hurt or neglect her. Feeling belittled is a wonderful compass to know when it is time for me to go inward and privately BE my *little* me—in order to cleanse out or shift old pain and replace it with new *big* love.

The person or situation that brought up your feeling of belittlement simply mirrors you back what is already in you— what is ready to be felt, dealt with, shifted, and healed by you. The fact that you are feeling it means that it is high time, because your *little* you might be neglected and ready to be cared for. It also is a clear sign that you are showing up as not-aligned with who you are right now—little, versus big. Once aligned, the belittling either stops - the mirror is unnecessary - or what others say, do, feel, or think won't be a thing for you anymore.

Answering any belittlement with your anger towards the mirror would not only undermine their purpose for you, but also create unwell-ness in and for you—making it an unhelpful response. Instead, this calls for gratitude for the diligence in bringing up this healing and happifying opportunity for you.

If you can't say thank you, that is fine. At least get yourself into a smiling space where you can send them an energetic memo in thought. This works wonders, because energetically we are all connected at all times. In theory you can always create the highest form of harmony for you and for the other person—no excuses!

I want to say, "Thank you to all 'belittle-ers!' You made, and still make, my day because I am healing, happitizing, and filling my little girl with love, at light-speed.

However, I never endorse any belittling! Bullying is never OK. Fact is, the 'belittle-er' IS crossing boundaries! End of story. So back-off!

Be kind. Be smart. Be helpful. Be real. *Be a good person!*

FEELING POWERLESS

Powerless-ness only exists on a physical life level!

Why?

Because on the soul level and in the energetic space of consciousness, there is only power—wisdom that is power, and a knowing that is power.

When you feel powerless:

• You are forgetting what the biggest part of you IS—energy!

• You are forgetting who you really are—an energetic essence!

• You are forgetting what you are here as in this physical life—a soul being!

• You are forgetting the power of what you have—a soul guidance!

• You ARE experiencing only through your physicality—forgetting to use your true soul power!

You ARE a soul being that is energetically wired with the possibility to always be plugged in and connected to the universal energetic space of "everything is possible"—an infinite and limitless essence of power. When you feel powerless, it's like your soul-alarm goes off for you saying, "Hey, you are not being the power that you actually ARE!"

When feeling powerless, instead of grasping desperately for power - or worse, convincing someone of your power by defending or explaining - take immediate action through shifting yourself to BE and live in your soul essence. Meditating, visualizing, or journaling of how your powerful you looks and feels, is a great way to claim your power again. Powerful breathing exercises, a power walk, or anything that pumps your strength is a job well done too—creating a sacred time in which you can recommit and refocus passionately about who you really are.

Are you feeling your power creeping back into your whole being again?

Realize that it actually never left!

The power leaving is an illusion—at least on the energetic level. Your soul essence, your power, is always wherever you are and always available for you to plug into and BE and live. The "creeping back" is really just firing it back up or plugging it back into connection—getting yourself all excited about being yourself again.

In reality, it is the most amazing happening ever because it's like a remembering, re-birthing, re-choosing, and like a re-committing of your always present and available super-power.

Important! Any form of powerless-ness resulting from any type of abuse is never OK. Get yourself - or the person in need - all the help. Don't hold back to speak or scream for help until you are heard.

Be kind. Be smart. Be helpful. Be real. *Be a good person!*

MY VOICE IS NOT HEARD

If this is the case for you, I think you should become louder—in your inside, your soul essence, and your soul-voice, by really really *really* connecting and feeling yourself as the huge energetic non-physical you that you ARE. Then… Let's talk about "not being heard" again.

"But what about my physical voice?" you might say…

Sure, you can become louder and louder in volume physically but if you are timid in your energetic voice, or your soul-voice is non-existent because of your dis-alignment, your physical voice will only be a physical "beep" and won't have the energetic force attached to it—hence, "I am not being heard." Being louder or more "yeller-like" in physicality while being tiny in energy is exhausting and a constant fight for being *louder* and *heard*. This is a hard way indeed!

The first real step here is to become energetically gigantic and louder by connecting to your powerful soul-essence, and then seeing if your physical voice still needs to go up a notch. You might find that there is no need for *louder*, after all, because your voice now has your energetic force powering it. And if by any chance you still want to, by all means get louder. More power to your voice!

Here is a great meditation - one that I mention in different variations thought the book - for you to connect to your loud inner voice:

Place yourself in a quiet room where you can BE and feel comfortable, safe, and open to whatever is coming in and up for you. Amp up the cozyness with candles, essential oils, pretty lights, and all things that light you into your glowing you—opening your female heart, your love portal!

Sit or lay, and cuddle yourself into a state of comfort

to start breathing in and out deeply. Every breath in is welcoming your absolute relaxation into a wholesomeness of "nothing," and every breath out you let yourself go further and feel as you are floating deeper into that beautiful "nothing-ness."

Once you are in that blissful state, focus on your soul-voice—its strength, power, wisdom, wideness, big-ness, sledgehammer-ness, and its volume. Breathe into that.

Ask questions like: How loud are you? How loud do you want to BE? How big are you? How big do you want to BE? How can I hear you better and how can I speak you louder?

This wisdom is yours to feel and heal, and to shift it into being your unquestioned knowing.

End this precious time with gratitude and love, and let yourself travel back into your now. Do this gently and with an unhurried agenda.

Breathe, and feel how you shifted as your woman into wholesomeness, knowing, enjoyment, and hopefully incredible excitement to trot down the street in your new day as your powerful female YOU! Time to get going, and move through your new NOW!

Give your soul-voice the space - in and for you - that it is here to occupy. Then feel, BE, and live it even bigger, even louder, and more clear because where you thought that your limit is, your capabilities are just starting. Limits are an illusion! You are limitless and your voice strength is limitless and the energetic space where you are originating from is without boundaries, rules, or limits. Consciousness IS infinite! Keep expanding and calibrating by being in alignment with the voice that you really are—ever vibrating, moving, and shifting to a loudness and clearness at all times.

To all the "I can't hear you" people, you have physical ears so start hearing even the tiniest of voices. They are here to be heard—no matter the volume of noise.

And to all voices, "I hear you... And you sound powerful!"

Be kind. Be smart. Be helpful. Be real. *Be a good person!*

THE FEELING OF BEING TAKEN
ADVANTAGE OF

First off let's be clear, we are talking about the *feeling* of being taken advantage of and not the actual act of being taken advantage of. If someone is taking advantage of you, get help and get out! Besides being hurtful on the physical life level, it is never an optimal space for your energetic expansion to BE and live in such a state, especially not for an extended period of time. You are not here in this physical life to stay in such a way of existing. You are here to shift yourself to BE and live into betterment, and more betterment, and more betterment.

Like me, it might be that you came forth to experience this type of exposure and then break out of it in order to expand in a certain way—to use that gained awareness to help others. But I believe that nobody is ever meant to have the soul journey of staying stagnant and forever in an experience of use or abuse. Everyone is meant to get out of it at some point. I never endorse being taken advantage of or taking advantage of anyone in anyway. Get help and get out—and step up for others who need your help.

Feeling taken advantage of can stem from old and gunky recordings of being used in your past, of witnessing someone that has been used or abused, or of an overlapping energetic essence from all of consciousness or past lives that you are carrying over into this life and are obviously supposed to feel, shift, and heal in this lifetime.

An interesting twist to this, is that this feeling can absolutely be created through you using and abusing yourself, too.

For instance, when you are running your soul being empty and into a non-connection in order to get something manifested or created in your physical life, "I'll do whatever it takes!" is the perfect sentence that should alarm you when it leaves your precious lips because you literally are squeezing the joy of being alive out of your energetic essence. Balance is key here!

Or when you are spiritually so connected that you sit days and days in meditation with your sweet soul being, yet, you forget that you also have a physical body. One that you are not moving for all those solar days—it will hurt getting up, I promise, especially when you are a bit more advanced in age. Balance is key here!

Of course a low amount of self-love, self-respect, self-appreciation, self-acceptance, and self-gratitude, play a role in this too. It all goes hand-in-hand. However, the reckless act of you using or abusing yourself plays the main role here.

Since this *feeling* of being taken advantage of is many times deeply imprinted in your internal hard drive, it is hard to kill. Usually I don't use such strong words, but I have a pun… Have you ever tried to kill a hard drive? I recently did by accidentally pouring wine all over my laptop—the hard drive survived. That is how hard it can be to shift the *feeling* of being taken advantage of into betterment if you don't know how and if you don't consciously heal it—you will carry it over and over into your next day and further on into next year, without ever stopping. Eventually you will go even further by blaming others for its existence, making a nice big mess while at it.

This is why I am writing about it in my book. I want to put focus on this feeling—to let it come up, to give you the opportunity to claim it, cleanse it, and shift it to betterment for yourself. Hopefully it will leave—good riddance!

Here are the steps:

• It's time to take responsibility of all of your feelings! No matter the what, where, why, and who, nobody can ever make you feel anything—instead, they can only tickle what is already in you to come up and show itself. Your feelings are your own unique decoration of your life, they are your personal style and preference. Just think how you feel about a song and how different someone else listening to the same track will feel. It is very personal. **Own your feelings and change the decoration they provide if you don't like them.**

• Acknowledge, accept, respect, appreciate, thank, and love all your *feelings* of being taken advantage of as a sign to realize how far off you stand from being aligned with who you really are. In connection with your true self you will never feel like that. Do whatever it takes to get yourself into your sacred space of being your soul you—and a beautiful and healing shift will be accomplished. From there - if you can - make peace with the person and the happening too. This heightens your expansion and calibration. If that is not possible for you right now, not to worry, you realized a fantastic expansion and calibration by doing what was necessary for you to feel better. Bravo!

The authority-move of taking control of how and what you feel means you take charge of yourself, create dominance in your life, and practice a mastery of your power—through which you guarantee that old unfitting feelings are free to come up, are acknowledged judgement-free, and will be cleansed out swiftly with the celebratory vibe that they deserve.

Fact is that, without something coming up and being acknowledged, nothing can ever be cleansed. Just think if the dust-bunny under the sofa is not showing itself, you can not acknowledge it's existence—you can't get rid of it. And that is that!

Be kind. Be smart. Be helpful. Be real. *Be a good person!*

SERVING OTHERS IN OVERDRIVE

Gosh, we are such good, serving beings! But is it really good for us?

It is known that just the word "woman" and the fact of "being a woman," has direct correlation to the word "service" and the act of serving. Just the picture of a woman, the physical being of a woman, and the sound or plain sight of a woman shifts one to feel the energetic essence of serving. This might sound strange, but it has been like that for a very very long time—resulting in very old beliefs, habits, and recordings. Then again, some history buffs say women used to rule whole villages.

I have to say, the latter is much more tasteful to my heart - and I trust that is for you too - than the fact that the expression of *woman* is a straight shot to *serve*. But we women are so over this whole old wives' tale of a woman's place automatically relating to that of a servant.

Or, are we not?

Well that depends on us women most and foremost. Hold your horses here, I know that this news is hard to swallow, but hear me out! I do have a point, promise!

Are we or are we not ready and able to move our focus beyond what IS and shift ourselves, how we look at ourselves and other fellow women, and feel our femininity, back to the time when women did lead villages—but in today's modernized way?

Are we willing to go into the state of denial of everything that IS going on right now, in us and around us, and do whatever it takes to radically focus on standing tall and proud as the female energy we promised to BE and live when choosing to come forth into our physical lives as such?

Are we feminine enough? I could say powerful but feminine and power ARE the same energetic value... To let everyone and everything that is not behaving accordingly to this women-are-not-servants-movement off the hook—because we know that they simply still treat the same old rusty mill and have not caught up with the news that their mill is about to crack and be replaced by a modernized, flashy, new mill? Of course, abuse as a way of misbehaving is excluded in this.

Are we ready for all that? If that is a "YES!" then we are in fact beyond that woman-equals-a-servant time, because how we show up IS the only thing that matters in order to BE and live in a time where women lead the world and villages—in a modernized way.

Change is an inside job first, and always starts with the one who wants the change to radically BE. Then, that one, goes on BEing and living the change with the determination that the change IS already a fact—"It IS that way now!" Think of an activist wanting to change the use of plastic. First it's an inside job of commitment, that the activist wants this change, then that person is BEing and living said change as a fact—this activist is not using plastic anymore.

Without these "first and foremost steps" you are looking at:

• Not understanding the fact of "everything is energy," of the energetic universal forces, your whole being and its power, and that everything is always firstly created inside of you by BEing, living, feeling, and thinking it.

• Not understanding that everything is old news after it happened—and that you are keeping the old alive and going by re-thinking, re-feeling, re-expecting, re-living, and re-behaving like a servant. Fact is that your next is always new—meaning you can always make a better new.

• An empty shell that is without the crucial aliveness that gives birth to something—physical action as a shell is good but energetic alignment to fill the shell makes worlds change.

• No stamina to make that "better new" permanent because without the soul-clarity the momentum will be lost over time, and become too tiring.

• Whatever you are desiring to change stays as a constant fight against the what IS, because solutions on the physical life level are limited, whereas energetically there are no limits. Truth is that when you are dis-aligned you are very stoppable—but aligned you are unstoppable.

Now do we want the female energetic essence of serving completely wiped out forever? No, of course not… I mean if you do, go ahead. For me as a mom and holistic practitioner, I love to serve when it feels good for me.

Serving from a strong feminine frequency is a wonderful and gracious act of caring and love. Just think of serving your husband, serving your children, or serving a dear friend, in sickness or in health—a fulfilling deed because it initiates in the power of femininity, not of being a victim or being ordered to serve.

Serving from a misaligned place of who you really are can turn into a "have to" scenario very quickly through which old gunk and history will repeat itself. Lashing out, losing it, and forgetting that some of the serving is actually very beautiful can be forgotten—all serving will be of unwell feeling. By then all joy is lost in the service department.

It boils down to holding yourself as the woman that you are and only serving from an aligned frequency. Nobody can mess with it that way. Plus, if they do, you know that they are still exhaustingly treating their old rutty mill. Poor them!

Something about personal time…

Make your private time rock-solid and not to be interrupted. If the interference is strong and won't give up - kids, husband, family, pets - ask yourself, "Does it feel good, that I am giving up my time for this disruption?" Don't tell your loved ones that I just called them disruptions and certainly never call them that out loud. Fact is that when you think of them as disruptions, your emotions about them become more self-centered towards you, meaning you can ask this question with less emotional baggage—like guilt, pain, and sometimes even love. You will receive a more truthful and aligned answer that way.

If the answer is "Yes, it feels good," then by all means, be interrupted.

If not, tell them to go away. "Later, not now!" Remember their feelings are theirs to feel, you are simply helping to get them to their surface by staying true to yourself. You can never make a person feel a certain way and vice versa.

If in any case you already did give in and are already interrupted but then don't feel good about it, learn for next time. Staying rock-solid is the point here!

Stay in your power and in your femininity! That is what you came here to BE and live.

Be kind. Be smart. Be helpful. Be real. *Be a good person!*

WOMEN, WEAK?

Really? Let's Think Again!

Many times the picture of a woman stands for petite, weak, dainty, gentle, soft, and all that gorgeousness that we are supposed to be made of. Whereas in truth, we are very strong, not all petite, super powerful, not always gentle, sometimes also have un-soft skin or hair, and we ARE made to grow humans inside of us and then give birth to them!

Picture this:

Think about a woman standing next to a man—feel the different energies. Usually the woman is being graciously feminine and the man the strong muscle. It's easy to picture that, not necessarily always good-feeling, but pretty automatic. Yes, I know, there is that one or the other Disney princess that is a warrior-leader, celebrated by all as a strong female, and it's so thrilling for our girls to see that. But I am talking about ancient beliefs and recordings and how the world put a stamp on how men and women have to be. Historians say that started after the time when women lead villages as leaders.

Back to picturing that "normal" woman and "normal" man standing next to each other...

Think about that same woman again. This time, visualize her giving birth. Imagine her all sweaty, going through the extreme pain of the contractions and pushing as hard as she can to give her baby the chance to take the first breath. Very powerful situation!

Now imagine that same man standing next to her while she is giving birth. This time the energetic reading is very different. The woman is now felt as super-strong, a strength that carries universal power, an unstoppable energy that worlds are made of. Whereas the man seems the weaker one in this, compared to the woman. You even hear men saying that they don't know how women can come up with the endurance of giving birth, that they could never do it or go through it, let alone withstand it.

We are talking about the same woman and the same man that we pictured standing next to each other, but now they are in this birthing situation. How in the world did this woman change from weak to strong overnight? Think about it, it's all in our heads and how we observe it, and on what old bull-poo-poo we are building on.

You would never say that men are weak because they can't give birth. Instead, it is just taken as a fact of physicality that they can't. It is not about strength because if men would be physically outfitted the same as women, they could do it too! That is the same for women not being able to physically do as men—women are not weak, just different in physicality. For equality purposes jump to the chapter **Starting out as Equals**.

My point is that if you feel that you are not strong or strongly living your life, it is because you are using the old imprinted ways that were stamped on your forehead many eons ago. The funny thing is that it was not true back then just as it is not true today, but today you have the chance of knowing better and changing to a modernized way of how you see yourself.

It all starts with women—with you!

You have to realize that you are the one who is seeing, feeling, sensing, hearing, tasting, smelling, and thinking of yourself in old ways first—spreading and sharing your old energy to everything and everyone out there. Them catching on to it and treating you as such, also based on their old beliefs, is just a side effect of it all. A mountainous one, that is!

Not saying that their old and untrue behavior is OK, but I want to bring into light that the change from "women are weak" to "women are equally strong" starts by you sharing the energetic essence of "women are equally strong" with every breath and step you take, moving forward in your life.

When people's actions make you feel weak, it is your strength barometer that is kicking in by you feeling miserable and weak. Take action by acknowledging your feelings, and by accepting, respecting, appreciating, thanking, and loving your feeling-signals as a great reminder of your misaligned power of your femininity and your whole being. Most likely you were re-filling the old belief bucket over and over—and drinking from that old and cloudy water all along. Stop that, it is indeed very unhealthy!

I want to take it even as far as saying, "show gratitude," silently or loudly, to the one that is mirroring you how weak you are showing up as! At the end that person is simply co-creating with you.

Abuse is a whole other case though, and it never fits this - or any - bucket or chapter.

Be kind. Be smart. Be helpful. Be real. *Be a good person!*

NOT DOING WHAT I WANT TO DO

Where is all that whining coming from? Who or what is keeping you away from what you want to do? I sure hope that your answer is not, "It's because I am a woman living in a man's world."

Even though it has some truth on the physical life level, why would we want to give this physical idea reason to live when we know that in energy we are all equal and in energy is where our ultimate power lies?

Have you ever watched how mothers do the seemingly impossible when their children are in danger?

What is keeping you from doing the same—from doing the impossible when your connection to your soul being is in danger of becoming non-existent? Forgive me, I love to be a bit dramatic sometimes because it sounds so much bigger and better that way, and I think it has more impact when I tell you that your best and biggest friendship - to yourself - is about to go into extinction. Yikes!

I say BE the hero and save yourself! Do whatever it takes to nurture your connection to your energetic essence and then go do whatever it is that lights you on fire. Know that nobody - not even men - can pour enough water onto your flames to put out that firey-hotness that you are.

If in any case your fire does go out, it is because you lost your conscious focus on keeping your connected fire going. Alert, you are about to go extinct again! That is where the miserable feeling of "I am not allowed, and am not free or able to do, what I want to do in this world because I am a woman" sneaks up on you—which is not true, as explained in this whole book over and over.

Claim your fire, because you ARE a soul being that is outfitted with the wisdom of your soul guidance, here to enjoy your soul passion, creating an impeccably fitting soul journey that you are here to experience.

Are you ready to walk your walk? Even if only sometimes it's in togetherness with others but a lot of times it's you alone—just you for you?

When it's a crowd, focus on your fire and allow other people's fire - if fitting! - to make yours even higher and hotter. When it's just you, realize that you don't have to share dessert with anyone. Life is an ever-changing event, it's supposed to shift from alone to together and back to alone. So don't try to stop this natural course, rather stay focused and tend to your fire. The rest, take it as it comes, one flame at a time, while doing what you want to do! Celebrate your perfectly burning fire by reminding yourself that your fire has it all—to make you faster, bigger, stronger, and more powerful.

No need for other people's flames. You can do whatever you want to do as your fiery-you, even in a man's world.

Be kind. Be smart. Be helpful. Be real. *Be a good person!*

IS NEAT AND PERFECT YOUR THING?

Many times the gorgeous existence of femininity comes with a profound need of perfectness, neatness, and something happening exactly as you want it to—especially in your living quarters.

While, many times out of worry, false responsibility claiming, or even controlling, putting yourself and your needs way at the end of the line for others, your loved ones, your job, or even a phone call that ends up being a telemarketer.

This behavior is not something that gets less with growing into wife-hood, motherhood, or when coming further into woman-hood—at least, until you are past 50, and then you don't care about what your surroundings are up to anymore. "Too busy being me," you will say!

For the ones saying, "That's not me!" because you practiced an "I don't care" mentality starting at an early age and never let it go, more power to you! Then again, that pesky need might be right at your doorstep just waiting to come in. However, since you have a heads-up, you can relax because its appearance won't catch you by surprise. You're welcome!

If the fabulous "I don't care" mentality has not come around for you yet, I got you covered—keep reading. Roll up your sleeves and let's get working.

When was the last time you held your pee because there were emails to be sent, dishes waiting to be washed, food to be cooked, people to be reminded of chores, or something else was of more importance than your bodily needs? When was the last time you felt that your people were not cleaning up after themselves the way you want them to? And when was the last time you thought that nothing is as perfect as it should be, as you want it to be?

A second ago, you say?

Woman, you are in trouble... You are infected with the widespread virus of femininity—the bug called PNEAIWI. **Perfect, Neat, Exactly As I Want It**.

The remedy to get it out of your system is a formula I have listed for you below. It lets you walk yourself through the steps before you *really* pee in your pants or create a painful state with real physical consequences—ouch! Not to mention, it helps you get out of your habits of doing everything for everyone just so it fits your style of perfect and neat.

Here it goes...

First, acknowledge the situation, "I am not farting because I am standing in a room full of people." Ha! Made you laugh... Now even though this situation is a suppression of your body function, it is most likely the right thing to do. Let's choose another situation. You are not peeing because you are too busy to get the preparations for the arriving dinner guests finished into perfectness, neatness, and exactly how you want it to be. That right there is a wonderful example.

Then, ask yourself:

• Is what I want to be perfect and neat a life-and-death seriousness or am I fabricating it to be the highest mountain—when it really only is a teeny-tiny ant hill? Is sticking up for my wantings and controlling the situation making me feel better, safer, and happier as a whole being? In other words: is the dinner-preparation of being 100% finished, that dirty plate in a room, or the email still needing to go out, a life or death situation? If the answer is no, you know what to do. If yes, then by all means avoid the killing! In the case of the plate, make the owner remove it—or at least claim the hero-throne if you end up saving the day by doing it yourself. Send that email and celebrate the completion. Or perfect the dinner party while peeing in your pants and bravely tolerating the created pain, knowing that it was a royal move to save lives. Point is, if it's a yes, celebrate yourself as a hero—creating incredibly high-for-life energies in and for you, and accomplishing a balance for any unwell feelings that might sneak up on you by your choice of priorities.

• Am I in my aligned place, a state where my needs as a whole - body, mind, soul, consciousness - are a priority? Am I making my choices from there? Or am I residing in a disconnection where everything and everyone but me are my priority—a state in which unwell feelings prosper? Is my inner me in agreement with doing "this" while putting my needs aside? Is my soul being happy with putting all my effort into this? Or would another way feel better for me?

• Am I clearly stating to myself and others, and am I giving crystal clear vibes, on how it has to be and why it has to be that way—this certain thing that I am putting above all else? Or am I playing hot potato with the hot sauce to not have to play big—to not have to justify my wishes and choices? Did I make a real hot fire under everyone's behinds or did I only start a teensy tiny flame? In the example of the email: Did I clarify to the recipient that the email would come when it comes—when it is perfect for me?

These are questions pumped with real answers, and the clarity they bring might surprise you. You will in fact see just how much of your precious energy you are wasting on old ways, on unclear messages, and unreal have-to's of your perfectness and neatness. They shed a bright light on all your efforts to make everything and everyone happen—followed by an uncovering of unwell feelings. Funny thing is that from the start, it never had anything to do with anybody else than you and your old ways.

Moving through this formula shifts you to accept the invitation to laugh it all off until you are in the fantastic "I don't care" mentality. You'll catch yourself more and more letting things slide and letting yourself and others off the hook, creating absolute freedom. Breathe into that, dear woman!

The result will be that everyone gets to relax because your idea of perfect and neat has changed to a freer version of living a perfect and neat life. If you have a family, they will gladly meet you there, saying "Finally!"

Which brings into the spotlight that the trouble-makers were simply giving you the opportunity to relax into letting go, being free-er, and enjoying a lighter you. They were mirroring to you what was already a deep desire in you, and probably had been for a very long time. If this makes you shed a tear, let it flow. It's part of the process. Beautiful!

It always IS firstly about you—and for you!

Now, don't give up all of your perfect and neat, I don't want you to turn into a slob… Instead, keep all the well-feeling perfect and neat habits. You know, the ones that make you happy—embrace them and feel your energize-ment because of the true-lifestyle you are BEing and living. Bravo!

Important! Check in with your "neat and perfect" often as it changes—because you change too.

Be kind. Be smart. Be helpful. Be real. *Be a good person!*

I GIVE, AND GIVE, AND GIVE

But when is too much, too much?

When your act of "giving" does not feel good to you, when you are already drained as-is, or when you feel drained after sharing—that is when too much, is way too much, and you have already crossed - at least with one foot - from "too much" into "my sharing is unhealthy."

Everything that goes out has to BE first—meaning, everything you give has to be available in energetic essence first in order for it's existence to be given. Either you create it by being aligned with your energetic limitlessness or it has to come in as a reception from your surroundings or from others.

"I give, and give, and give… and nothing ever comes back!" is a bomb of a sentence that should have you in the readiness of saying, "Enough!" not to others, but to yourself, because you are oversharing yourself. Not in a social media oversharing way - although there maybe too - but in an unhealthy draining way. You are oversharing your energy and are giving what you have not aligned with or you don't have.

When it does not feel good for you to give, it's important to take that seriously and believe your unwell feelings. They are your truth barometer!

To get to the bottom of the "why" ask yourself the following:

- Am I already drained or empty?

- Am I feeling drained after giving?

Take your answers and run with them by radically embracing this wisdom and matching your style of giving to what is right for you—to make "giving" a feel good experience for you.

When you are already drained, find what is draining you, and find where you are giving your energy away or too much. Is it the latching onto other's negativity, the gossiping, or giving too much focus to the world news? Is it that you are not taking beautiful time-out time, sleep, for yourself? Is it that you are not putting any effort into energizing yourself by practicing alive-ness for your whole being––body, mind, soul, consciousness? Put a stop to these energy-sucking moments and ways! Be unapologetic about it.

Everything you give that is resourced from an under-filled cup makes what you have left even less for you. Think of sharing your under-filled cup of tea—leaving not even a sip left for you to enjoy, or imagine sharing a sprinkle of chocolate... That one hurts my heart to even think about. Bottom line is, what's left for you is not much and not enough! Not a satisfying state to BE and live in or show up as.

If you share from a full and overflowing cup, what you share still leaves enough for you. The overflow won't even tickle your awareness of how much energy you are sharing—you don't need or have use for your overflow. It's up for grabs.

When you are feeling drained after giving, even though you start out feeling really good, know that there is no energetic exchange happening. It's like a one-way conversation, you talk and nothing comes back, not even an echo. Result being, drained feelings like being used, abused, made feel less, disrespected, not taken care of, not loved, not appreciated, and "It's always me..." mix themselves into your act of giving. An unwell feeling combo indeed.

If that is the case, ask yourself: "What is the *void* of that missing energetic exchange?"

"Am I giving because I freely want to?" If not, you will feel drained after giving.

"Am I giving because I have to?" "Am I giving to make things happen for someone—or else it won't be?" "Am I giving because the person is very needy—yet very capable of doing it themselves?" In all of these types of giving, you will feel drained.

"Am I giving because that is how I - or the receiver - measures how much I love them?" A dangerous and very inaccurate measurement. Love is always a feeling and not an action! Any action that is done to get love-results is of impure nature, energetically and in physicality.

Important! The missing exchange that I am mentioning here has nothing to do with the idea that "if you give, something has to come back, or else you stop giving." Giving should always be without the expectation of receiving anything in exchange. The missing exchange that I am bringing up here, is the *void* that you feel when your giving is not of the truest and most purest nature for you—when it's not a well-feeling act. I want to make sure that you are in your purest essence when you give out your gracious donations of your wholesome being—to keep your energetic cup full and overflowing, healthy and as it supposed to be. A happy giving indeed.

Be kind. Be smart. Be helpful. Be real. *Be a good person!*

STANDING UP FOR YOURSELF IS NOT WORKING

The question I have for you is, "What are you aligned with when you stand up for yourself?"

Being that it is a significant moment, when you stand up for yourself, it matters infinitely if you are using your full power to get your point across.

Does your "standing up for yourself" come with the added benefit of your fully aligned whole-being-sledgehammer?

Your two essences - physical and energetic - have very different possibilities of performance, and therefore different outcomes are only normal. Standing up for yourself from only your physicality has limits, whereas energetically you are limitless. Combine the two, and you are indeed unstoppable and not able to be stood down.

My three "W" questions are immensely truth-showing and help me even in the most dire moments. They only take seconds to ask and answer, a real plus since most of the time you only have seconds to decide the best way to stand up for yourself.

Here are the three "W" questions:

• Who's boss right now, your physical or energetic essence?

• Which part has the better of you right now, your physicality or your energy?

• Who are you mostly right now, your physical or your energetic power?

Practice asking these questions, and even consider using a stopwatch to time yourself. How fast you can feel yourself into your alignment? Have some fun with this!

To explain more in depth:

Are you standing deeply connected, tall and proud, clean and pure, rooted and rock solid, limitless and infinite, and happy as can BE in the big fat middle of your energetic soul being? In a space where your whole power lays, and through that you advocate for yourself in your physical life—where you are being and experiencing from your biggest part and greatest power?

Or are you only standing as your physical being in your wholeness of physicality - a space of real limits without your deep soul-wisdom - and are standing up for yourself from there?

Clear signs as to where you ARE show themselves as the following:

If your standing up is from alignment, people will take your set boundaries and you feel well in the process. You got it right—to the universe's delight. Keep going!

If your standing up for yourself is not working, nobody's listening, or nobody's respecting your newly set rules, it is a given that you are not aligned as a whole. Rather, you are solely in your physical essence and are pushing back as that limited entity.

This standing-your-ground malfunction is a gift! It is a sign that you are not the complete power that you ARE. It's a great chance for you to shift into yourself, your whole, and then revisit the situation fully powered-up. Who knows, you might find that the situation is not even there anymore, because when you shift, people shift too. If still present, try your standing up for yourself maneuver again. The outcome will be different!

If it's the case that while you get firmer in who you are and how you push back, your surroundings struggle or throw tantrums, know this will pass. Keep your alignment strong and keep pushing forward. Their reactions are theirs to feel, shift, and heal.

If you notice that your loved one's lives start to have more problems because of you standing firm for yourself, take this as a great sign that you are indeed expanding to a fabulous new you and are calibrating as such to who you really are. Their lives will relax again once they own their own power too—which you are so wonderfully demonstrating to them. Stay in your new firmness and don't be tempted to shift back into your old ways.

To all the annoying people, things, and situations in your life - past, now, and future - that offer you the gift of standing up for yourself: "Thanks for the generous deed!" Just think where you would be without them—most likely not where you are today.

So next time you are standing up for yourself, with a skip in your step make absolutely sure that you are feeling, seeing, hearing, tasting, smelling, sensing, thinking, and are acting from your newest plateau of alignment—which, keep in mind, changes every split second of your physical lifetime.

If after a while you find that you don't need to stand up for yourself as often anymore because things are smooth rolling, know that this is a reaction to you being and staying aligned in your highest power. People will know better than to mess with you. Congratulations!

This brings up the fact that if you have the itch to stand up for yourself, it starts with you not being in your fullest and highest power—and that is why the need for others to test you arises.

No harm done!

Simply shift into your full power and then from there ask yourself, "Do I really have the need to educate them about my powerful-me, or do I rather do something else, like flashing my powerful teeth as a smile at them?" Because you know that this testing of you will disintegrate as soon as you are your power again—it was never about them but all along about you.

Go with what feels right for you and with the preservation of your wholesome energy in mind. Feeling good is always what counts!

Be kind. Be smart. Be helpful. Be real. *Be a good person!*

ARE YOU A FIXER?

Silly question! More often than not if you are a woman, you are a fixer—it's imprinted in the being-ness of femininity and comes naturally without you even realizing it, until your loved one says "Stop fixing me!" That is when you go "What??? I just wanted to help..." and the feeling of being a stabbed animal arises.

Where does this fixer personality come from?

When you think about the energetic pool of consciousness, it has been going on since ever and ever—women are home, taking care of everyone, helping and fixing everything for everyone.

It's even called "fixing dinner" for crying out loud! Funny, what was there ever to fix in dinner anyways? I bet this comes from women always doing the fixing—from holes in pants and socks all the way to meals. Of course if there is a bad cook involved it would make sense...

Almost every woman carries the essence of "fixing"—an automatic feeling that keeps the already existing wave going and going. But there is another side. If you are a perfectionist, which many women are, then you are fixing things and people just so you have it your way—so you can feel good or better.

Wanting to fix things and people also means that you are coming from a belief that something or someone is broken, bad, needs to be fixed, needs to be better, or even is wrong. What a broken old belief that is—definitely in need of fixing since nothing is ever wrong, but always only IS. There can also be a hero-flavor of "showing up as the ONE that fixes the world" present—not ideal since the physical world does not need fixing, but rather alignment is in order.

Being a fixer - for others and for yourself - comes with issues, unwell-ness, exhaustion, and the consequence of missing the point attached. You bring whatever it is that you want to fix to a stagnancy. Just think, have you ever tried to fix someone - or something - and they completely blocked? Seems normal since their energetic essence and the universal force knows that there is nothing that needs fixing. Besides that, fixing brings momentum into what you want to change, making it bigger and bigger with a lesser possibility for it to really change while in that big-ness. A better way is to realign with your energetic essence where change can be initiated - since everything always firstly IS energy - then show up to BE and live as that change, as it already IS a physical reality.

I am a natural fixer who converted into a natural shifter by putting my fixer-feature to its best use—at my work it comes in handy to know how to create shifts - fixes, if you will - because my clients, students, and readers want me to help them change. This never results in fixing, though, but rather in understanding what IS, and through creating a shift moving on to a more gracious NEXT. It changes everything for people, because they calibrate to their fitting solutions which result from the understanding that there is never anything to fix— rather only to align, and align, and align.

Imagine the extra energy you have available when you let go of your fixer nature, and shift it into a great well-feeling mechanism, like I have. You will be this energizer bunny who creates a better fitting NEW without ever stopping. Way to go!

In my book **Parenting Through the Eyes of Lollipops** I speak about fixing your children... There is never anything to fix there either. For more on this pick up a copy, or two, or three. Heck, gift them to anyone you know!

Be kind. Be smart. Be helpful. Be real. *Be a good person!*

That, my dear woman, concludes what I know and understand, AM and live, love about, and want to share with you about **What it Means to BE a Woman**. I truly hope that you ARE taking every new breath and new step forward in your female existence as your true power—to pave the way furthermore for yourself and for every new woman there will be.

So you can say as your whole being and from your whole heart, "I lived my woman in my physical lifetime to the moon and back, and beyond—it could not have been any better!" once it's your glorious time to transition.

I see you!

I hear you!

I feel you!

I know you!

I think of you!

I AM you!

I love you!

Yours truly,

Jacqueline

Dear Woman, or man if that is so,

You made it! I hope you enjoyed this book as much as I loved writing it. If you did, it would be wonderful if you could take a short minute and leave a review on Amazon.com and Goodreads.com as soon as you can, as your kind feedback is much appreciated and so very important. Thank you!

I also want to let you know that I wrote two other best-selling books: *365 Days of Happiness*, a day-by-day guide to being happy, and *Parenting Through the Eyes of Lollipops*, a guide for parents to get cracking on "mindful parenting"—a supportive tool for parents and a clear voice for children. Both support the teachings of *What it Means To BE a Woman* and help people, parents, and children to BE and live happier—a cause that is very dear to my heart.

All my books are available wherever books are sold, online on amazon.com, amazon-worldwide, and at www.freakyhealer.com. *365 Days of Happiness* is also available as a companion mobile application for both Android and iPhone, and can be supplemented with the appropriate self-study program that you can find at www.freakyhealer.com.

For any question you might have and for more information on my sessions, workshops, presentations, and what ever else I am up to, visit my website www.freakyhealer.com and my social media accounts @freakyhealer

Thank you again for enjoying and supporting my work. You mean the whole bar of chocolate to me.

Yours,

Jacqueline

ABOUT THE AUTHOR

Jacqueline Pirtle is the owner of the lifestyle company FreakyHealer. She is a holistic practitioner, a speaker, and a bestselling author. Her books, *365 Days of Happiness*, *Parenting Through the Eyes of Lollipops* and *What it Means to BE a Woman* represent her passion for mindful happiness which shines through in all areas of her life and work helping clients to shift into a high-for-life frequency—a unique experience that calls people into their highest potential in their NOW!

Jacqueline has been featured in multiple online magazines, including Authority Magazine, Thrive Global, NBC NewsBetter, has appeared on Women Inspired TV, and interviewed on radio shows such as The Sunday School Radio Show, The Lisa Radio Show and WoMRadio. Her article "Are You Happy?" is in print in The Edge Magazine.

Jacqueline was born in Switzerland, has lived all over the world, and now makes her home in the US with her phenomenal family. Her professional background is in holistic wellness and natural living, she holds various international degrees, and is an internationally certified Reiki Master. She also considers herself a professional red wine and dark chocolate taster.